FRAME IT!

FRAME IT!

by
The Vanessa-Ann
Collection

Meredith® Press, New York

For Chapelle Limited

Owner: Jo Packham
Staff: Trice Boerens, Gaylene Byers, Holly Fuller, Cherie Hanson, Susan Jorgensen, Margaret Shields Marti, Jackie McCowen, Barbara Milburn, Pamela Randall, Jennifer Roberts, Florence Stacey and Nancy Whitley

Designers: Rett Ashbey, Trice Boerens, Gaylene Byers, Tracey Carrera, Brian Hammond, Mary Jo Hiney, Donene Jones, Pearl and Richard H. McCowen, Jo Packham, Jennifer Roberts and Flo Stacey.

Photographer: Ryne Hazen

The photographs in this book were taken at Mary Gaskill's Trends and Traditions, Ogden, UT and at the home of Jo Packham. Their friendly cooperation and trust is deeply appreciated.

Meredith® Press is an imprint of Meredith® Books:
   President, Book Group: Joseph J. Ward
   Vice-President, Editorial Director: Elizabeth P. Rice
For Meredith® Press
   Executive Editor: Maryanne Bannon
   Senior Editor: Carol Spier
   Associate Editor: Guido Anderau
   Copy Editor: Barbara Tchabovsky
   Production Manager: Bill Rose

ISBN: 0-696-02384-9
Library of Congress: 93-077501
First Printing 1993

Published by Meredith Press

Distributed by Meredith® Corporation, Des Moines IA.

10 9 8 7 6 5 4

Printed in the United States of America.

All of us at Meredith® Press are dedicated to offering you, our customer, the best books we can create. We are particularly concerned that all of the instructions for making projects are clear and accurate. Please address your correspondence to Customer Service Department, Meredith® Press, Meredith Corporation, 150 East 52nd Street, New York, NY 10022 or call 1-800-678-2665.

Dear Crafter,

Whether it's a fine painting, a favorite photo, or a treasured memento, when you mount a piece of art in the perfect frame, you'll instantly enhance both its aesthetic appeal and its value. Beautifully framed art adds a wonderful finishing touch wherever it hangs— in a formal living room, whimsical child's bedroom, quiet hallway, or even kitchen or bath. And there's absolutely no need to visit a professional framer. In fact, unless a piece is truly valuable, you can easily frame it yourself— and give it an appropriately romantic, witty, funky, casual or tailored look.

FRAME IT! provides full color photographs and complete instructions for making over 60 different frames, each with limitless possibilities for individual interpretation, and each an expression of personal style. There's even a helpful Basics section to get you started, and full-size patterns wherever needed.

For any work of art, photo, piece of stitchery, or bit of ephemera you may wish to treasure, you'll find an idea for framing that is just right— to present and protect it, for yourself or friends and family, to keep it in their hearts and yours for years to come.
Sincerely,

Carol Spier
Senior Editor

Table of Contents

Table of Contents

Chapter Two

Table of Contents

Chapter Three

INTRODUCTION

A frame is the final step in the creation of a painting, a drawing, a piece of needlework, or a much-loved photograph. A frame enhances and sets the artwork off from its surroundings. In addition to its aesthetic functions, a frame protects the artwork from physical damage and deterioration. Art of any kind is susceptible to damage from handling, from dust and moisture, from mold, and even from atmospheric pollutants.

A good frame and mat should complement a picture or work of art without overpowering or detracting from it. That does not mean, however, that the frame and/or mat cannot be as much a work of art as the piece being framed. The entire piece—art, mat, and frame—should become a cohesive unit, ready to be displayed.

A century ago, the Impressionists not only shattered art tradition in their paintings but also defied tradition in their framing. They selected simple white frames in place of the ornate gilded frames used by the masters in the previous century. The turn-of-the-

century artist Georges Seurat felt it necessary to change tradition even further. He continued the image of his painting off the edge of the canvas and onto the frame itself. The American painter James Whistler was so convinced that the frame was as important as the art itself that, to prevent patrons from removing his simple frames in favor of gilded frames many people considered more impressive, he handpainted his frames with complementary patterns and signed each one with his butterfly trademark, thus making the frames as valuable as the art inside. American portrait painter, Thomas Eakins, framed his portrait of Phillips Academy science professor Henry Rowland with ordinary flat boards. On them he carved the scientist's own notes. Eakins considered this to be the perfect frame for this particular painting.

Today, in framing your art, your may want to duplicate the frames and mats you see in this book, or you may use this book as a springboard and with your imagination create an original—a frame that is unique and the first of its kind!

General Instructions

Choose a Frame Appropriate to the Art

In addition to being appropriate for the art, a frame should also be solid and sturdy. It should be built to protect the piece and to last for generations. Rules for framing are made to be broken—until you find the right frame for your particular piece of art. Nonetheless, following some principles about the kind of art, its era, and the environment in which it will be displayed can ensure success. All properly framed pieces have certain elements—frame, glass and mat (if desired), art, mounting board, back paper, and hanger. Each part is described in more detail on page 16.

Pictures painted with oil or acrylic are usually on canvas stretcher bars, canvas-covered boards, or hardboard. When choosing frames for oils and acrylics, be sure they are deep enough to conceal the stretchers. Generally, these pieces are not covered with glass unless extra protection is needed. Similarly, needlework and fabric art are usually stretched over hardboard and may be framed without glass. Fabric pieces need to breathe and, if framed with glass, will need to have a mat and an open edge on the back to allow for changes in the environment.

Pastels, because they smudge easily, need the protection of a mat, maybe even a double mat, in addition to fixative and glass. Photographs lend themselves to inventive framing depending on the image itself, and they are usually covered with glass. And today, posters and prints of all kinds are available. Those with strong graphic content may look best in simple frames. Fine watercolors, drawings, old documents and prints need museum-quality mounts (discussed on pages 12 and 13) and glass to protect them from dust. Functional art, such as a map or diploma, is often best displayed with a simple, narrow frame.

Three-dimensional art calls for extra care in the selection and preparation of a shadow-box frame that separates the glass and the backing with enough space to highlight the three-dimensional aspect of the piece.

Certainly, there are circumstances in which you will want to take a piece to a professional framer, but much of the time, art can be framed and matted artistically and securely by anyone who has the inclination to do so. All that is required are the appropriate materials, a few special tools, a little imagination or a good idea, a complete set of instructions, and the desire to do so. This book gives numerous ideas for frames and mats, some very easy to do, others a bit more difficult that might be easier to complete with a little assistance from a professional.

Framing art yourself does not just save money. Designing and constructing a frame can be both fun and rewarding. A piece of art is chosen or created because of what matters to you—the emotional appeal, the colors, the textures, the lines—qualities that are part of your personality or appeal to you. The same can be true for a frame. Using the innovative and eclectic ideas in the pages of this book, you will be able to design the mat and frame that are perfect for your art. You can have frames that are visually strong or subdued, complicated or plain, painted or stained, traditional, Victorian, contemporary, or country.

Planning

In selecting the perfect frame and/or mat for your art, you should consider how to aesthetically integrate the picture with its surroundings and how, at the same time, to integrate the shape, color, texture, and size of the mat and frame as they relate to the art. For some pieces of art, a large mat or a double mat may be the best choice; for others, a small mat or perhaps no mat at all is best. Consider the effect you want to achieve (quaint, sleek, or ornate), choose the basic type of frame you want (wood, metal or acrylic), and then try to visualize the art, the mat, and the frame as a cohesive unit.

Before Beginning

You will need to have some basic tools and supplies on hand in order to create any of the projects shown in this book. Most of these you probably already have, those you do not can be purchased at your local variety, hardware or crafts supply store, or the lumberyard. Before beginning, assemble a variety of rulers, scissors and craft knives, glues, pencils and other markers, tracing, carbon and scrap paper, sandpaper, assorted paintbrushes and palettes, paper towels and rags. Work in a space that is well-lighted and ventilated, and on a surface that is appropriately protected for the cutting or painting process you will be using.

A few of the frames featured in this book are to be made from purchased moldings. You may wish to adapt some of the stock moldings sold in lumberyards or hardware stores; however, some woodworking experience is helpful when doing this and you may need a miter box (or a table or radial arm saw), a router and a lightweight drill. Most frame shops will be glad to order moldings cut to your specifications and many provide workshops for their customers where they can cut or assemble custom pieces themselves, at a savings.

Mats can be purchased precut—be sure you have accurate outside edge and window measurements— or you may want to purchase large pieces of mat board and cut your own.

Measuring

Accurate measurements are the key to a successful project. In this book, measurements are given to match the model in the photograph and, in most cases, you can adapt our project to fit your art. First decide how much of the art you want to reveal, or, in other words, the cropping. This gives you the dimensions of the window of the mat (if using one) or the frame. Next, figure the dimensions of the outside edge of the art or the mat, which need to extend into the rabbet or lip of the frame. In this book, all measurements given are for the front of the finished product. In other words, if the window on the frame is 8" x 10", the art or mat will be 8½" x 10½" which is ½" wider and longer than the frame window. This difference allows the art or mat to extend into the rabbet. It is important that your measurements include the area hidden in the rabbet.

Ready-made and custom frames make this accommodation and are sold by the outer dimensions of the mounted art; in other words, purchase an 8" x 10" frame for an 8" x 10" photo.

Purchasing or Assembling a Frame

Before purchasing or assembling a frame, be sure to check the measurements of the art. Then, decide if you want or need a frame with glass. Choosing to assemble your own frame opens a wide range of possibilities. Strips of stock molding can be glued and clamped together into a number of shapes, sizes, and combinations. If you are cutting moldings yourself, be sure to sand and clean them appropriately before gluing.

A clamp is essential. An angle clamp enables accurate and efficient positioning of molding pieces to make a 90-degree corner. You may also use a bench vise or C-clamps. Apply wood glue to the cut surfaces of two adjoining ends to form the first corner, allowing the glue to bleed outside of the seam. Place both sides in the clamp, tightening slightly until the corner is joined. Wipe away excess glue. If the molding is delicate, pad the clamps to prevent damage.

Reinforce the corners with small nails through the thickest part of the molding, drilling first to prevent splitting. Then, use a nail set to recess the heads. Hide nail holes with wood filler that matches the molding. Sand carefully, if needed. Repeat these steps one corner at a time, making sure all corners are right angles.

Decorating a Frame

Before you begin to decorate or individualize a frame in any of the ways described in this book, there are several preliminary steps. First, if the frame has a glass, remove the glass and backing before doing anything to the frame. If a frame is to be painted, it should be clean. Use fine sandpaper to smooth all rough edges and brush away grit that remains. Some frames may need to have an old finish removed or filler added to rough spots. After you have completed decorating the frame, mount the art and replace the glass and backing. The use of glass is often optional. (In this book, it was almost always omitted because of the glare it can create in photography.)

Cutting Mats

Mat boards are not only decorative: they also protect the art from coming into contact with the glass when framed. Mat boards are available in dozens of colors, textures, and patterns. If your art is valuable, choose acid-free products. If it is important that the finished mat have a beveled edge, it is probably better if a professional cuts the mat. But, for mats that are to be covered with fabric or paper, you can cut your own.

The tools you will need are a metal straightedge and/or ruler, a sharp craft knife, a kneaded rubber eraser, and a pencil. The surface of mat board is delicate; handle it carefully.

Begin with a piece of mat board that is slightly larger than that which you will need for the finished

project and, before measuring, check the corners to be sure each is a right angle. Correct, if necessary, when marking the cutting lines. On the front of the mat, mark the outside dimensions. Then, mark the window.

Place the mat on a cutting surface. Place the straight edge on the marked line. Be sure you are working with a new, razor sharp blade. Beginning and ending exactly in the corners, make a score line. Then repeat with gentle cuts until the blade penetrates the mat board; this may take six to ten times. After cutting all four sides, the center should fall out. You may need to sand the edges with an emery board, always working in one direction.

Conventionally, mats are cut 2½" to 4" wide, but you need not be bound by any rules. Experiment with the proportions. Other options include multiple mats. In planning your measurements, cut the innermost mat first and all outside edges exactly the same. Allow at least ¼" of each mat to show. You may elect to have more inner mat exposed or uneven amounts if there are multiple mats. Secure the mats together with double-sided tape.

Mounting Art

Art is mounted in several ways, depending on its value, type, size, and other factors. Always place a mat between valuable art and glass to prevent damage from trapped condensation.

Paper Art: Mounting paper art requires a stiff board, such as foam board, heavy mat board, or illustration board. Spray adhesive used according to the manufacturer's directions is the method most commonly used to mount paper art of transitory value.

Dry mounting is another technique for mounting paper art. This method, which should be considered permanent, is particularly appropriate for small projects (8½" x 11" or smaller). It requires a special mounting tissue available in photography shops and a household iron. Again, follow manufacturer's directions.

Delicate or valuable works of art should be handled more carefully. Only the top two corners of the art should be secured to allow for minimum attachment and unrestricted movement. The art should be attached to the mounting board with acid-free, adhesive-backed linen tape. To make a hinge, cut two short pieces of tape. Place one, adhesive side up, perpendicular to and part way under art. Tape the extending portion to the mounting board with the other piece of tape (adhesive side down). The art can be removed without damage to it by cutting in the centers of the hinges.

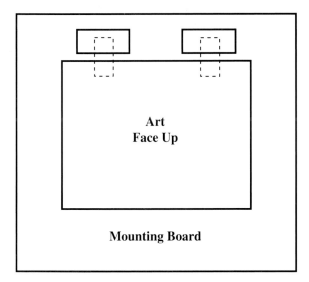

**Art
Face Up**

Mounting Board

HINGE DIAGRAM

Another accepted method for securing art is to use acid-free corners. Corners can be made from Japanese paper or can be purchased.

Fabric Art: Framing fabric, tapestries, or needle-work involves different techniques. First, the fabric must be stretched.

Stretching is done by lacing or stapling, but delicate pieces like silk should always be laced. Begin by determining the grain of the fabric and trimming the edges along it, allow 3" or more extra on all sides to wrap to the back. If the art you want framed does not have this extra material on all sides, sew muslin strips to the edges.

For lacing, cut a mounting board slightly smaller than the size of the rabbet of the frame. You may want to pad the front of the matting board with a layer of fleece. It softens the appearance of the art. Place the piece to be stretched face down on the work surface, center the mounting board, and fold the excess fabric to the back of the mounting board. Secure the fabric on the grainline with pins (Diagram A). Fold corners flat and slipstitch (Diagram B). Using a strong thread and large needle, lace from side to side (Diagram C and D). Working backwards, pull the lacing taut; secure ends. Repeat on opposite sides. Be certain to check often to make certain the piece is being pulled evenly.

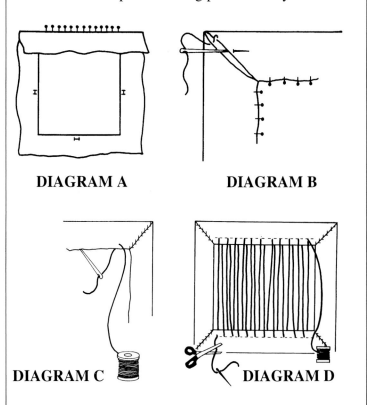

DIAGRAM A   **DIAGRAM B**

DIAGRAM C   **DIAGRAM D**

For stapling, staple the fabric to stretcher bars or a mounting board made of foam board sandwiched and glued between two pieces of mat board. Foam board by itself should not be used since it may bow under the tension of the fabric. Make certain that rust-proof staples are used and that the staples are not too long for the stretcher bars or mounting board. Place fabric face down. Center stretcher bars or mounting board. Wrap fabric around to back and begin stapling, working from the center of one edge out as with lacing above. Check your work often to make certain the fabric is being consistently and evenly stretched. Do not skimp on staples. When inserting staples, make certain they are at an angle and do not always fall between the same warp or weft; this will weaken the fabric. Be careful not to tear the fibers. Fold corners so they lie flat.

Needleart or fabric, if possible, should not be framed with glass. If glass is used to protect the piece from soil, the fibers should not touch the glass. The piece must be ventilated from the back. With a paper punch, put two holes in each of the bottom two corners of the backing paper. This permits the humidity inside the frame to fluctuate with its surroundings and prevents deterioration.

Hanging the Framed Piece

Most pictures are framed so that they may be displayed on a wall, but pictures can also be framed in a free-standing easel frame and displayed on a table or shelf.

The most popular method to hang a frame is to use two eyescrews attached to the backing and a braided wire. Smaller pieces can be supported by a sawtooth hanger, centered on the top edge. Select your supplies, which are available in a variety of sizes, based on the size and weight of the framed piece.

Attach eyescrews one third of the way down from the top of the frame. Be sure the eyescrews are not too long for the molding. Loop wire through the eyescrews, leaving a 3"-to-4" tail to wind back around the main length of the wire. If the framed piece is very heavy, the piece may be supported with a loop of double wire wrapped through several eyescrews.

Arranging framed art attractively on a wall or the mantel does not just happen. It is done with careful consideration to the environment in which it is placed. Generally, art that is framed is hung is at eye-level. In a hallway where people will be standing, the framed pieces can be higher than in a den. Give careful thought to heating vents and sunlight in a room because direct contact with either can be damaging to certain types of art.

Grouping framed pieces calls for special attention to proportion and shape. To achieve a harmonious grouping in a room busy with patterned fabric and carpet, you may want to frame unlike pieces of art in frames that are alike or similar in design. Other rooms can handle a mixed assortment of shapes and sizes, of colors and styles, even of old and new. One way to test an arrangement is to place the pieces on the floor as you envision them on the wall and experiment. Pay special attention to the space between each piece, making it narrow enough to keep the framed pieces a unit and wide enough to avoid having them interfere with one other. Once arranged, evaluate the lighting of the pieces, perhaps adjusting the lights and lamps in the room to accent particular works.

Making a Stand

Although there may be some variations depending on the exact nature of the frame and how it and the art are to be displayed, there are certain general guidelines for making a stand.

1. Cut a rectangle from the mat board. The measurements for this piece are given in the Materials list and the Directions for each frame in which it is needed.

2. Mark and cut one end of the mat board to about two-thirds the width of the opposite end (Diagram 1).

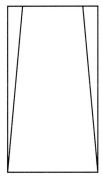

DIAGRAM 1

3. On the wrong side of the stand, score a line half way through the mat board ¾" to 1" below and parallel to the top, narrow edge (Diagram 2), making a hinge.

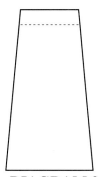

DIAGRAM 2

4. Cover the stand. For this step, refer to the Directions given with each frame; you may cover the stand with fabric, wrapping paper, or other material.

5. Glue the stand (above the hinge) to the back of the frame (Diagram 3).

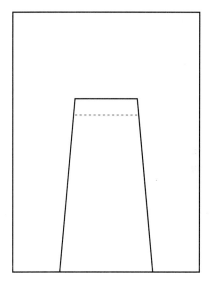

DIAGRAM 3

6. Glue one end of the ribbon (listed in the Materials list) 1" above the bottom, wide edge of the stand piece.

7. Glue the second end of the ribbon to the back of the frame 1" above the bottom edge (Diagram 4).

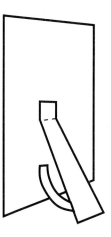

DIAGRAM 4

Basic Terms

Frame: Both decorative and functional, the frame creates a border that defines and protects the art. It is built from molding. The molding has a rabbet—a lip to support the glass and mat. Molding is available in a wide variety of styles, widths, and finishes.

Glass: Glass is not essential for frames, but it is relatively inexpensive and protects the art. It is usually $^1/12$" thick, thinner than window glass, and easily cut to size. Because glass can create condensation, which, in turn, can damage the art, it should be kept away from valuable needlework and art by a mat. Nonreflective glass is available, but it may dull the colors and textures of the art. An acrylic sheet (such as Plexiglas®) may substitute for glass, especially on very large pieces, because it is lighter. It does not create condensation and may be placed directly against the art. On the other hand, acrylic scratches easily and yellows over time, and wiping it creates static.

Mat: The mat is a thick layer or layers of paper board that provide "breathing room" between the frame and art—a "frame" within the frame. Mats are available in dozens of colors and in many textures. Most have a white core, but some cores are buff, black, or other solid colors. The color that shows around the window when the mat edge is beveled can complement the art. Although a mat is optional, it holds the glass off the art and, should there be any condensation, it will affect the mat rather than the art. The best mats are made of acid-free paper.

Art: Almost anything can be the "art" — even three-dimensional works. The mat and the frame should enhance the individual characteristics of the art. In all cases, the art dictates the frame and not the reverse. It is the art that the viewer should notice first, not the frame or the mat.

Mounting Board: Hidden inside the frame is the board—hardboard or craftboard—against which the art is held. A photograph or poster may be mounted permanently onto the board, while a rare or antique piece should be hinged against an acid-free material. The mounting board (with the mat and glass, too, if used) is held in place in the frame with brads or staples.

Back Paper: Usually heavy brown paper, this layer seals the framed piece against dust and other pollutants. It is attached with double-faced tape or glue. Sprayed lightly with water, the paper will shrink and become taut.

Hanger: The hanger for a framed piece must match the weight of the item. Large pieces need heavy rings attached with screws and wire and perhaps even some extra reinforcement. Smaller pieces may use small eyescrews or just a saw-tooth hook attached with brads.

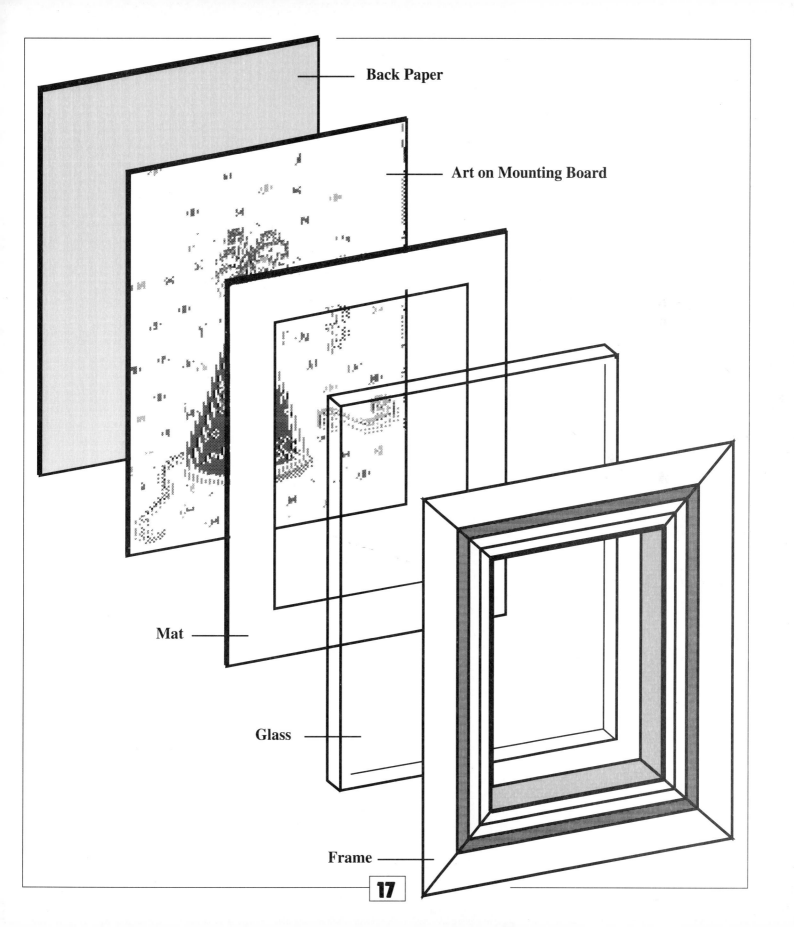

Back Paper

Art on Mounting Board

Mat

Glass

Frame

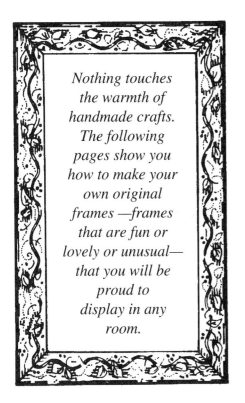

Nothing touches the warmth of handmade crafts. The following pages show you how to make your own original frames —frames that are fun or lovely or unusual— that you will be proud to display in any room.

ASTROLOGIE
GAULOISE

LE CHÊNE

Dominante physique : forte
Dominante intellectuelle : moyenne
Dominante affective : faible
Dominante sociale : forte

si vous êtes né le
21 mars

équinoxe de Printemps
vous êtes Chêne

Chapter One

Pencilled In

MATERIALS
Four new pencils
3½" x 5½" foam art board
1 yard of coordinating 1"-wide
    ribbon
Spray adhesive
Scissors
Tape
Hot glue gun and glue sticks

DIRECTIONS
1. Using spray adhesive, mount the art onto the foam board. Trim the edges flush and set aside.

2. Sharpen the pencils. The pencils need to be 2" to 2¼" longer than the corresponding edges of the foam board.

3. Center and glue one long pencil to each long side of the foam board, alternating eraser ends. Center the two shorter pencils on the short sides of the foam board, gluing lightly where each intersects with the pencil on the long side.

4. Cut the ribbon into four 9" pieces.

5. Carefully feed one piece of ribbon behind the top pencil on the left corner (Diagram 1). Crisscross the ends over the front of the pencil and wrap to back (Diagram 2) and knot tightly.

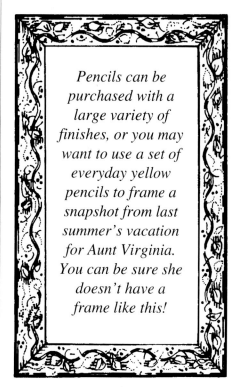

Pencils can be purchased with a large variety of finishes, or you may want to use a set of everyday yellow pencils to frame a snapshot from last summer's vacation for Aunt Virginia. You can be sure she doesn't have a frame like this!

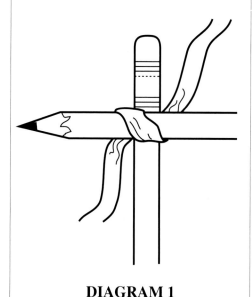

DIAGRAM 1

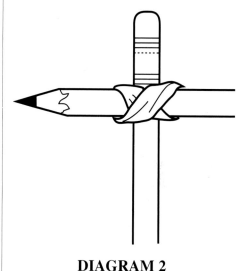

DIAGRAM 2

6. Trim the ribbon ends about 1½" from the knot. Tape the ends to the back of the foam board (Diagram 3). Repeat Steps 5 and 6 at the remaining corners.

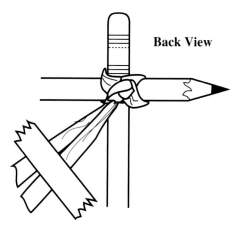

Back View

DIAGRAM 3

LE POMMIER

Dominante physique : faible
Dominante intellectuelle : moyenne
Dominante affective : forte
Dominante sociale : faible

si vous êtes né entre le
25 juin et 4 juillet
ou entre le
du 23 décembre au 1er janvier
vous êtes Pommier

Familière, candide et trapue, la stature peu imposante du Pommier charme et repose le regard. Les anciens nommaient « Paradis » une variété de l'arbre, quand l'épopée gauloise glorifiait votre fruit gage d'invulnérabilité. Le héros Condlé, fils d'un roi, sent, au terme de sa centième bataille, ses forces l'abandonner. Au déclin de sa défensive il lance un appel recueilli par la femme du royaume des ancêtres. Elle viendra vers le conquérant lasse par son rôle axial de communication d'une pomme impérissable, suffisant à l'appétit du guerrier mythique car se reconstituant aussitôt qu'entamée. Ce geste de don et d'amour nous rappelle que vous étiez, Pommier, sacré et relié à l'érotique et l'art d'aimer.

Le goût du plaisir, la gourmandise d'existence du Pommier est manifeste, sans ambage. N'exigons pas de vous des qualités de stratégie ou des calculs. Votre intuition, votre sensualité dépourvue de malice font de vous un être immédiat et généreux.

Dilettante, ce signe aime l'étalage. Cette soif peu ordonnée d'instruction qui l'anime par périodes vient à pic contrecarrer les caprices d'une mémoire pas toujours très sûre.

Amoureux de l'instant, badaud du réel et sentimental incurable, vous exigez, Pommier, mesure et prudence dans les décisions et les comportements. Votre défiance définitive de toute passion tourmentée peut, se dégrade en mollesse... voire en mélancolie.

Dans leur ensemble, les Pommiers demeurent trop hédonistes pour éprouver le goût, de pénétrer leur personnalité profonde. C'est avec ravissement qu'ils déchiffrent, dans le regard les paroles ou les attentions d'autrui, un peu de leur nature.

Faits pour l'amour, on attend beaucoup de ce signe. Nombre d'âmes tourmentées fréquentent le Peuplier, se consoler à l'abri de vos tendres charmes.

LE CHÊNE

Dominante physique : forte
Dominante intellectuelle : moyenne
Dominante affective : faible
Dominante sociale : forte

si vous êtes né le
21 mars

équinoxe de Printemps
vous êtes Chêne
carte

Imaginons, proche de l'actuelle Orléans, une forêt baignée d'une lumière profonde : la forêt des Carnutes. Là, se rendent rituellement les plus grands initiés des magiciens gaulois. Abrités par des hauts chênes, les religions et les sacrifices sont célébrés. Au pied des arbres divinisés, sanctuaire originaire, les tribus, qui jamais ne cessaient de s'affronter, plaidaient leurs différends et apaisaient leurs rancunes. Un Chêne royal, élancé, mythique et noble, élongeait ses ramures en une voûte de justice ombrant ce lieu où l'on pouvait pour un temps sans encombre rencontrer les Dieux. Sous sa protection, les secrets initiatiques se transmettaient aux futurs sacrificateurs et voyants.

Le Chêne est, en tout temps, synonyme de force. Solide et majestueux, épris d'équité, en vous correspond la période qui marque le réveil et le renouveau de l'ordre naturel. Aussi, vous inspirez confiance et respect. Intimidant mais apaisant, maître des arbres, le Chêne joue son rôle axial de communication entre le Ciel et la Terre mère. Adoré par les Gaulois, il était, par son large tronc et ses branches généreuses, emblème de l'hospitalité, l'équivalent d'un temple. La réelle noblesse du signe se révèle dans sa disposition remarquable à l'accueil.

Chêne, votre stabilité et votre ténacité sont vos meilleurs atouts. Grand seigneur épris de faste, vous aimez recevoir, éblouir, ordonner à autrui divertissements et obligations. Énergétique, autoritaire, excessivement fidèle à la parole donnée, votre indépendance est loin d'être toujours sereine. Lorsque l'idéal très élevé que vous aimez inscrire au faîte de votre existence devient inaccessible.

Davantage, confiant en amitié, des phases d'abattement vous guettent lorsque l'idéal très élevé que vous aimez inscrire au faîte de votre existence devient inaccessible.

Avec l'âge, vous gagnerez à faire preuve d'indulgence envers vous-même et vos proches.

Cinnamon Sticks

MATERIALS

Four 8" to 9" cinnamon sticks
4" x 6" piece of foam art board
1 yard of 1"-wide ribbon in a
    contrasting color
Spray adhesive
Scissors
Tape
Hot glue gun and glue sticks

DIRECTIONS

1. Using spray adhesive, mount the art on the foam board. Trim the edges flush and set aside.

2. Center and glue one cinnamon stick to each side of the foam board. Glue lightly where sticks meet.

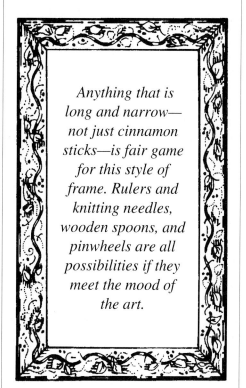

Anything that is long and narrow—not just cinnamon sticks—is fair game for this style of frame. Rulers and knitting needles, wooden spoons, and pinwheels are all possibilities if they meet the mood of the art.

3. Carefully feed one piece of the ribbon behind the top cinnamon stick on the left corner (**Pencilled In** Diagram 1, page 21). Crisscross the ends over the front of the stick and wrap to back (**Pencilled In** Diagram 2, page 21) and knot tightly.

4. Trim the ribbon ends about 1½" from the knot. Tape the ends to the back of the foam board (**Pencilled In** Diagram 3, page 21).

5. Repeat Steps 3 and 4 at the remaining corners.

Rustic Stick Frame

MATERIALS

One dark wood narrow frame with a
8" x 10" window
Straight green lilac branches: see
Preliminary Steps, Step 1 below
Jigsaw
Small sharp knife
One wood cutout: 2½" x 5½"
(e.g., a rabbit)
Walnut wood stain
Small wire brads
Wood glue
Hammer
Two 16-penny nails
Drill and ¹⁄₁₆" wood bit

DIRECTIONS

Preliminary Steps

1. Cut the lilac branches into the
following pieces. Be sure to notice
whether to miter or square the ends.

Quantity	Length	Width	Placement	Cut
3	9"	½"	Front	
2	10⅞"	½"	Front	
4	18"	½"	Front	
4	15"	½"	Front	
1	6"	½"	Stand	
2	15¼"	⅜"	Stand	
1	10"	⅜"	Stand	
2	11"	⅜"	Stand	

*Making this frame
is so easy that you
may want to make
more than one
while you have the
tools out. The
wood cutouts are
as close as your
craft store.
Experiment with
different shapes or
add some wood
stain to the sticks.*

2. Prepare the wood cutout for
painting.

3. Stain the cutout; allow to dry.

Decorate the Frame

1. Fit together two 9" and two 10⅞"
lilac pieces around the frame and,
using the small brads, nail these
sticks around the front of the frame
(see photo).

2. Center and nail one and then a
second 18" piece to one long side of
the frame, placing mitered corners
face-to-face (see photo).

3. Repeat Step 2 on the other long
side of the frame.

4. Center and nail two 15" pieces to
the bottom of the frame, placing
mitered corners face-to-face and
placing both sticks over the sticks
on the sides.

5. Repeat Step 4 on the top of the
frame.

6. Center and nail the wood cutout
to the remaining 9" piece, driving a
nail through the branch and into the
cutout.

7. Center and nail this piece with
the cutout to the top of the frame
(see photo).

8. Whittle the ends of the 6" piece
so that they are slightly rounded.

9. Drill a hole into each end of this
piece.

10. Glue and nail this piece to the center top edge of the back of the frame.

11. Mount the art.

Make the Stand

1. Place the 15¼" pieces on a flat surface. Mark point 1" from top mitered end on both 15¼" pieces. Position these two sticks so that they are 6" apart at the 1" mark and their square ends are at the bottom 8¼" apart (Diagram 1).

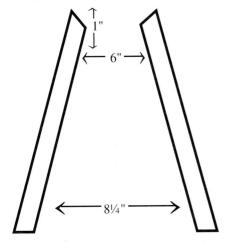

DIAGRAM 1

2. Glue and nail the 10" piece across the lower part of these pieces 5½" from the bottom (Diagram 2).

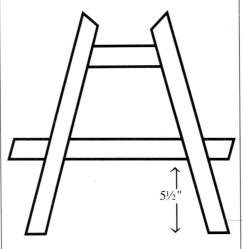

DIAGRAM 2

3. Glue and nail the two 11" pieces in a "V" (Diagram 3).

Drill hole at 1" mark   Drill hole at 1" mark

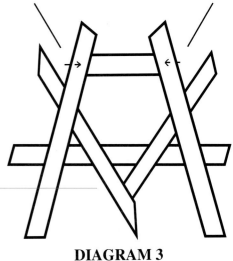

DIAGRAM 3

4. Drill a hole at 1" mark on each of the long side pieces.

5. Align the holes in the 6" piece on the top back of the frame with the holes in the sides of the stand. Gently hammer a 16-penny nail through each stand hole into the 6" frame piece; this makes a hinge for the frame and stand. Work until the tension is correct and the frame stands firmly upright.

Clearly Cool

Square Frame
MATERIALS

Two 5½" x 5½" pieces of acrylic
Two 4" dowels ¼" wide
Two 5½" x 5½" pieces of
lightweight cardboard
Glossy enamel paint: black
Paintbrush
12" gold elastic cord
Drill and ⅛" bit
Very small crochet hook
Double-sided tape
Masking tape

DIRECTIONS

1. Paint dowels with two coats of black paint; allow to dry.

2. Mark placement for holes on the plastic coating of the acrylic (Diagram 1).

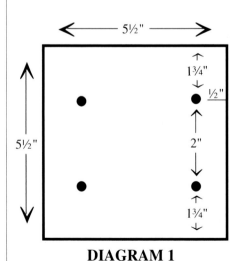

DIAGRAM 1

Acrylic frames can be used for pictures as well as for contemporary cards that may be works of art themselves. Traditionally, the holes and dowels would be hidden, but if your art offers an opportunity to incorporate these features, they assume twofold uses. You may have to make holes through the art, too— or make your own "art" from pretty paper.

3. Layer the acrylic with the marked side on top, then cardboard, second piece of acrylic, and finally, second piece of cardboard. Wrap masking tape around the center of the layered pieces to keep them secure while drilling.

4. Drill holes in the acrylic.

5. Remove the plastic coating from the acrylic.

6. Remove the cardboard and place the art between the two pieces of acrylic, anchoring the art on the back as needed with double-sided tape. Then, wrap with masking tape again.

7. Cut the gold cord into two 6" pieces.

8. Tie a secure knot in one end of one piece of gold cord. Hold the cord behind the top left hole. Reach through the hole with a crochet hook and catch the cord, pulling a loop through to the front and pulling the knot against the hole. Slide one end of a dowel through the loop.

9. Reach through the second hole on the left side with a crochet hook and catch the elastic cord, pulling a loop through to the front. Slide the other end of the dowel through this loop.

10. Working from the back, tug gently on the cord to secure the dowel. Then, knot the cord.

11. Using the other piece of gold cord, repeat Steps 8, 9, and 10 to attach the other dowel on the right side of the acrylic.

12. Glue hanging hardware to the back if desired.

Rectangular Frame
MATERIALS

Two 5" x 7" pieces of acrylic
Three 1¾" dowels ¹⁄₁₆" wide
Two 5" x 7" pieces of lightweight
  cardboard
Metallic gold paint
Paintbrush
1¾ yards of metallic gold braid
  ¹⁄₁₆" wide
Drill with ⅛" bit
Double-sided tape
Masking tape

DIRECTIONS

1. Paint dowels gold; allow to dry.

2. Complete **Square Frame** Steps 2, 3, 6, 4 , and 5, in this order, referring to Diagram 2 for placement of holes.

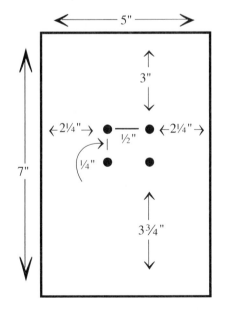

DIAGRAM 2

3. Cut the gold braid into four pieces: two 4" pieces and two 25" pieces.

4. Wrap one 4" piece of gold braid around the three dowels (Diagram 3), pull snugly, and knot ends.

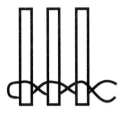

DIAGRAM 3

5. Place the wrapped dowels, with braid ends to the back side, on the front of the acrylic. Then, thread the second 4" piece of gold braid through the holes in the acrylic, making an X (Diagram 4), and knot on the back side.

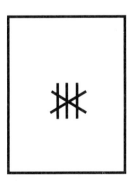

DIAGRAM 4

6. Wrap one 25" piece of gold braid around two diagonal corners of the frame and knot on the back side (Diagram 5).

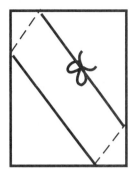

DIAGRAM 5

7. Repeat Step 6 above with two remaining corners (Diagram 6).

DIAGRAM 6

8. Glue hanging hardware to the back if desired.

Gabled Frame

MATERIALS

27" of ¾"-wide embossed molding
   OR two small frames made
   from the same embossed
   ¾ "-wide molding
One 3" x 5½" mat board
Craft knife
Paintbrushes
Acrylic paints: mauve, green
Acrylic spray paint: bronze
½"-diameter porcelain rose
½"-diameter round wood spacer
   ¼" thick
Wood glue
Spray mat varnish

DIRECTIONS

1. Using embossed molding, make one frame with a 2½" x 3½" window. Then, make gable (Diagram 1). OR, use one purchased frame as is and make gable from second one by cutting corner at 45 degrees.

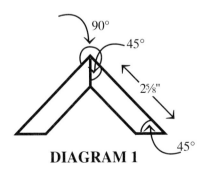

DIAGRAM 1

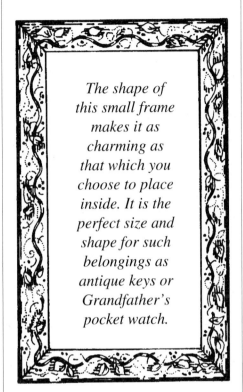

The shape of this small frame makes it as charming as that which you choose to place inside. It is the perfect size and shape for such belongings as antique keys or Grandfather's pocket watch.

2. Cut mat board into one 3" x 4" piece and into one triangular piece for gable, 1¼" x 1¼" x 1¾ "(Diagram 2).

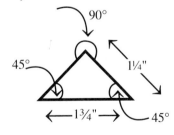

DIAGRAM 2

3. Center and glue the gable to the top edge of the frame (Diagram 3).

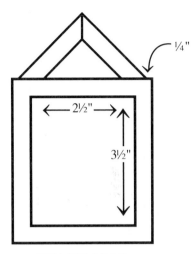

DIAGRAM 3

4. Paint the frame, gable, mat board, and spacer mauve. Allow to dry.

5. Paint the leaves or other embossed details in the frame green. Allow to dry.

6. Spray the painted surfaces with bronze. Allow to dry.

7. Paint porcelain rose or other embossed details on the frame mauve. Allow to dry.

8. Glue the gable mat in the gable window.

9. Glue the rose to the spacer. Then, center and glue the spacer to the gable mat. Spray with varnish; allow to dry.

10. Mount art on 3" x 4" mat board. Secure.

Santa Fe Style Metal Frame

MATERIALS

Mat board: two 5½" x 8½" pieces
    and one 4½" x 5½" piece
Craft knife or scissors for metal
One 6" x 8½" sheet of tooling brass
Small pieces of tooling copper
Epoxy glue
One 1¼"-wide purchased silver
    medallion
Two 1¼"-wide purchased copper
    thunderbirds
One ⅞"-wide copper octagon
3" piece of ⅜"-wide tan ribbon
Pencil
Tape

DIRECTIONS

1. Cut one Pattern 1 on page 34 without a window from one large piece of mat board. Cut one Pattern 1 with larger rectangular window from the other large piece of mat board. Use the small piece of mat board for the stand. (For directions on how to make the stand, see General Instructions, page 15.)

2. Cut one Pattern 1 with smaller rectangular window from the brass sheet.

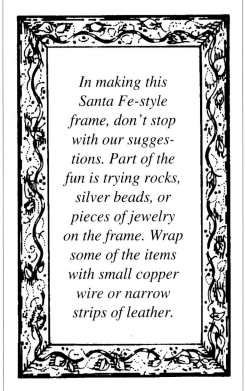

In making this Santa Fe-style frame, don't stop with our suggestions. Part of the fun is trying rocks, silver beads, or pieces of jewelry on the frame. Wrap some of the items with small copper wire or narrow strips of leather.

3. Cut one Pattern 4 on page 34 from the brass sheet.

4. Cut one Pattern 2 and one Pattern 3 on page 34 from the copper sheet.

5. Center and glue the copper octagon over the brass Pattern 4.

6. Center and glue the brass pattern with the copper octagon onto the copper Pattern 3 and then glue to the frame (see photo).

7. Center and glue the silver medallion onto the copper Pattern 2.

8. Center and glue the copper Pattern 2 with the silver medallion onto the frame.

9. Glue the copper thunderbirds onto the frame (see photo).

10. Glue the metal frame to the mat with a window.

11. With the side of a pencil, bend the window edge toward the back to make a beveled edge.

12. Mount art on the back of the mat and secure with tape.

13. With wrong sides facing, glue the mat without a window to the mat with a window.

14. Attach the stand.

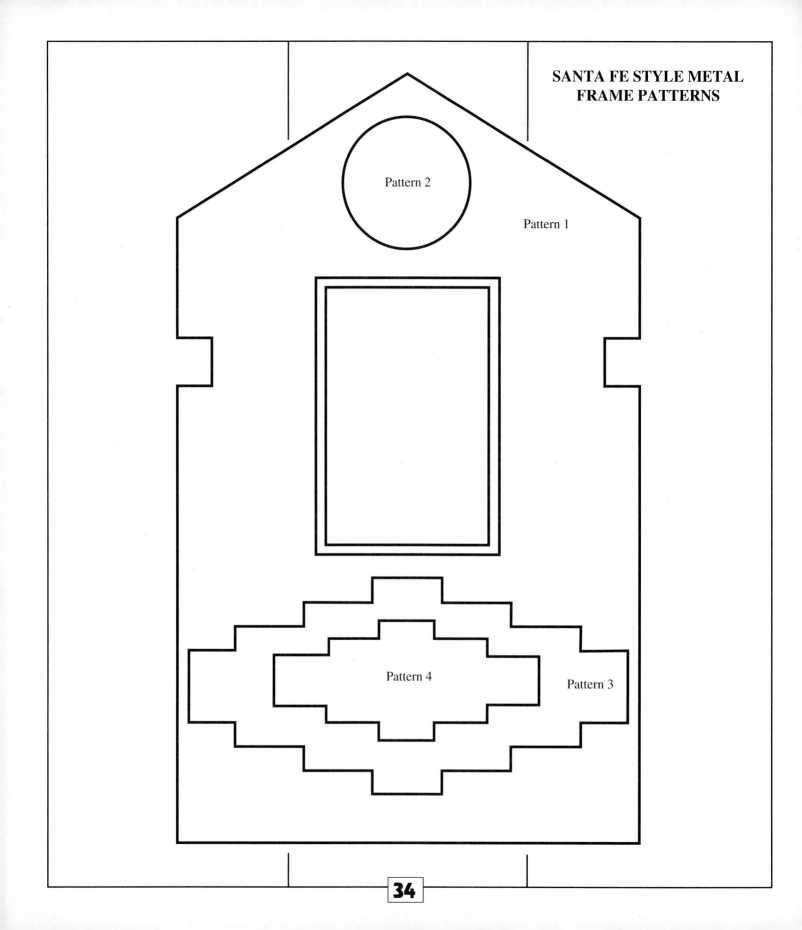

SANTA FE STYLE METAL
FRAME PATTERNS

Pattern 2

Pattern 1

Pattern 4

Pattern 3

Black Velvet Frame

Black Velvet Frame

MATERIALS

Mat board: two 12" x 15" pieces, two 2" x 15¼" pieces, two 2" x 8⅛" pieces, and one 9" x 5" piece

15" x 18" piece of black velvet

Dressmaker's chalk

Black felt-tipped marker

Spray adhesive

Craft knife

Scissors

Tacky glue

½ yard of 2"-wide black ribbon with gold dots

1 yard of ⅜"-wide gold scalloped trim

2 yards of ⅞"-wide black/gold trim

1 yard of a different design ⅞"-wide black/gold trim

One large decorative pin

Spray paint: gold (optional)

3" of ⅜"-wide black satin ribbon (for stand)

DIRECTIONS

1. Cut a 4" x 5" window and curved top on one piece of the 12" x 15" mat board (Diagram 1). Use the 9" x 5" piece for the stand. (For directions on how to make the stand, see General Instructions, page 15.)

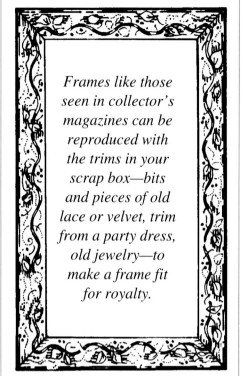

Frames like those seen in collector's magazines can be reproduced with the trims in your scrap box—bits and pieces of old lace or velvet, trim from a party dress, old jewelry—to make a frame fit for royalty.

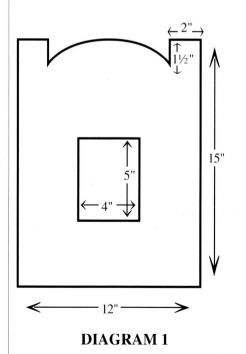

DIAGRAM 1

2. Color all edges of the mat boards with a black marker.

3. Place the velvet face down on a flat surface. Center the mat with the window on the wrong side of the velvet. Using dressmaker's chalk, trace all edges onto the velvet.

4. Cut 1" inside the marked edge of the window all the way around.

5. Spray the mat with window with adhesive and center on the velvet. Clip the corners nearly to the edge of the window.

6. Wrap velvet edges around the window to the back of the mat. Wrap the long edges of velvet to the back. Mitering corners, wrap the bottom edge to the back. On the top edge, clip the inside corners and curved edge to within ⅛" of the mat (Diagram 2). Fold the velvet to the back. Reinforce the velvet edges with tacky glue as needed.

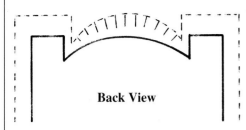

Back View

DIAGRAM 2

7. Cut the black dotted ribbon into two equal lengths. Using either tacky glue or spray adhesive, center and attach the ribbon to each of the two short mat boards and wrap the ribbon ends to the back.

8. Cut the scalloped trim into four 9" pieces. With tacky glue, attach the pieces to the top and bottom edges of the dotted ribbon on the short mats.

9. Cut the black/gold trims into six 18" pieces. Using tacky glue or spray adhesive, attach two like pieces on the edges of the long mat boards and a contrasting strip in between.

10. Spray the large pin gold, if desired.

11. Attach the pin to the center top of the mat (see photo).

12. Center and, using spray adhesive, attach one short mat piece below the pin. Center and place the second short mat piece near the bottom. Then, attach both long mat pieces along the side edges (Diagram 3).

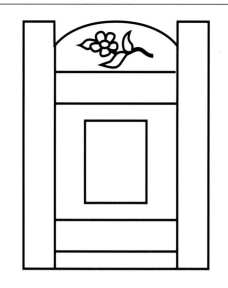

DIAGRAM 3

13. Mount art. Secure.

14. Glue the back mat to the back of the frame.

15. Attach the stand.

Tile Frame

MATERIALS

One 18" x 24" piece of ¼" plywood
13 feet of ¼" casing (lumberyard
   wood trim)
Saw
Small finishing nails
Hammer
Broken tiles
Grout
Acrylic paint: dark green
Paintbrush
Spray semi-gloss varnish

DIRECTIONS

1. Using the saw, cut a 12" x 18" window in the plywood base (Diagram 1).

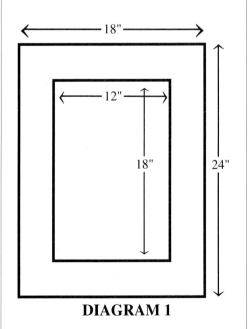

DIAGRAM 1

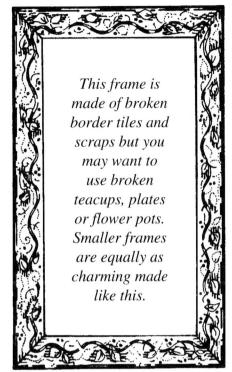

This frame is made of broken border tiles and scraps but you may want to use broken teacups, plates or flower pots. Smaller frames are equally as charming made like this.

2. Cut the casing into two 24" pieces, two 12" pieces, two 17½" pieces, and two 18½" pieces.

3. Nail the 24" pieces of casing to the long outside edges of the base and the 18½" pieces to the short outside edges. Be sure that the back edges are flush.

4. Nail the 12" pieces to the short edges of the window and the 17½" pieces to the long edges. Be sure that the back edges are flush.

5. Prepare the frame for painting.

6. Paint the casing and the back of the frame dark green.

7. Mix the grout to the consistency of peanut butter. Fill the frame front about ⅝ full with grout.

8. Place the broken tiles in the grout as desired. Fill in around the tile with grout as needed and then wipe off any excess. Allow to dry for two to four days.

9. Varnish entire frame; allow to dry.

Summer Reflections

MATERIALS

12"-diameter rustic twig wreath
    with 10" opening
10½"-diameter mirror
3 yards heavyweight craft wire
Hot glue gun and glue sticks
Sheet moss
Eight long stemmed dark green
    silk grape leaves
Three light green silk grape leaves
One bunch purple statice
One bunch dried mustard flowers
Seven silk roses
Three stems artificial berries
One bunch small white seed pods
One bunch long seed pods

DIRECTIONS

1. Cut the craft wire into six pieces, four 20" lengths, one 6" length, and one 12" length. Set aside the 12" piece for the hanger.

2. Lay the wreath flat and center the mirror over the wreath opening with reflective side against the twigs. Crisscross the 20" wires over

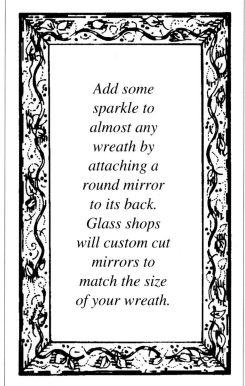

Add some sparkle to almost any wreath by attaching a round mirror to its back. Glass shops will custom cut mirrors to match the size of your wreath.

the mirror back (Diagram 1). Loop and twist the wire ends tightly around the thickest twigs on the wreath.

Back View

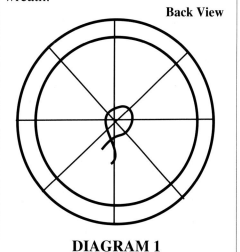

DIAGRAM 1

3. Twist the 6" wire around the center of the crossed wires (Diagram 1).

4. To make the hanger, double the 12" length of wire. Twist the ends around a thick twig of the wreath.

5. Turn the wreath face up. Press sheet moss down among the twigs, securing with glue as needed.

6. Glue the grape leaf stems around the wreath, alternating colors.

7. Glue other items to the wreath as desired (see photo).

Wrap It Up!

MATERIALS

10" x 13" mat board
Two mat boards of a coordinating
    color: one 9" x 12" and one
    9½" x 5"
12" x 15" piece of heavy wrapping
    paper
Craft knife
Spray adhesive
Scissors
Glue
3" of matching ⅜"-wide ribbon

DIRECTIONS

1. Cut a 6" x 6" off-centered window in the 10" x 13" mat (Diagram 1). Use the 9½" x 5" piece of coordinating mat board for the stand. (For directions on how to make the stand, see General Instructions, page 15.)

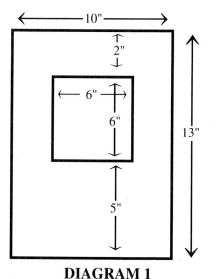

DIAGRAM 1

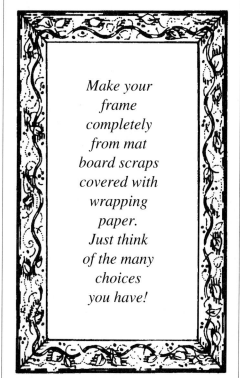

Make your frame completely from mat board scraps covered with wrapping paper. Just think of the many choices you have!

2. Spray adhesive onto the back of the wrapping paper.

3. Center the mat with the window on the wrong side of the wrapping paper. Wrap the paper to the back on the long edges and then on the short edges, folding each corner carefully to keep flat. Use additional glue in corners as needed.

4. With the frame still face down, place it on a protected surface. Using the craft knife, cut about 1" inside the window, all the way around. With scissors, cut diagonally into each corner nearly to the edge of the mat and wrap the flaps to the back side. Roll the paper with your finger to mold into each corner.

5. Mount art. Secure.

6. Center and glue the 9" x 12" mat to the back.

7. Attach the stand.

It's a Wrap

MATERIALS

Molding with smooth, rounded edge
   for one frame
Wrapping paper
Spray adhesive
Small, sharp scissors or craft knife

DIRECTIONS

1. Cut four molding pieces for
frame, mitering corners.

2. Cut wrapping paper wide enough
to wrap ½" to inside of molding and
½" longer than each end.

3. Spray adhesive on wrong side of
paper and on matching molding
piece.

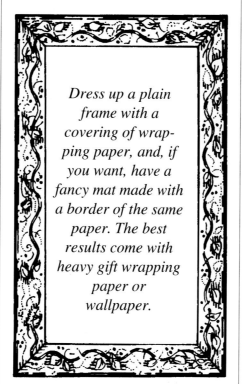

Dress up a plain frame with a covering of wrapping paper, and, if you want, have a fancy mat made with a border of the same paper. The best results come with heavy gift wrapping paper or wallpaper.

4. Center molding over paper and
roll, smoothing with hands to cover
surface. Wrap long edges to inside.
Trim ends carefully with scissors or
craft knife.

5. Repeat to cover remaining pieces
of molding.

6. Assemble frame.

Fabric Cameo Frame

MATERIALS

Mat board: one 5" x 7" mat piece, one 5" x 7" piece with oval window, and one 2½" x 4" piece

¼ yard of fabric

Dressmaker's chalk

¾ yard ⅝"-wide braid that matches fabric

½ yard matching thin cord

Spray adhesive

Hot glue gun and glue

3" of ⅜"-wide black satin ribbon (for the stand)

DIRECTIONS

1. Use 2½" x 4½" mat board piece for stand. (For directions on how to make the stand, see General Instructions, page 15.)

2. Cut the fabric into five pieces: two 7" x 9" pieces, one 4½" x 6½" piece, one 2½" x 4" piece for the stand, and one piece ½" larger than the stand piece on all edges.

3. Place one piece of the 7" x 9" fabric face down. Center the mat with the oval window over wrong side of the fabric and, using dressmaker's chalk, trace all the edges.

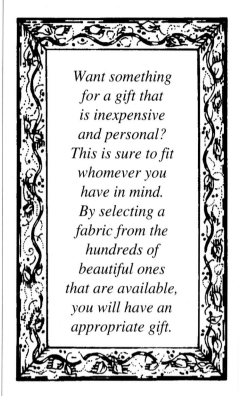

Want something for a gift that is inexpensive and personal? This is sure to fit whomever you have in mind. By selecting a fabric from the hundreds of beautiful ones that are available, you will have an appropriate gift.

4. Cut the fabric ½" inside the window all the way around. Then, cut perpendicular lines nearly to the edge of the window.

5. Spray adhesive on one surface of the mat. With the windowed mat centered on the fabric, fold the fabric tabs to the back and glue.

6. Spray adhesive on the wrong side of the second 7" x 9" fabric piece.

7. Center the other 5" x 7" mat board on this fabric. Wrap the fabric

edges to the back, clipping any excess fabric from the corners as needed, and glue to secure.

8. Spray adhesive on the wrong side of the 4½" x 6½" piece of fabric. Center on frame back, covering edges of the existing fabric.

9. Spray adhesive on the wrong side of the larger piece of stand fabric.

10. Center the stand on the fabric. Wrap the fabric edges to the back, clipping excess fabric from the corners as needed, and glue.

11. Spray adhesive on the wrong side of the stand fabric piece. Center it on the stand, covering the edges of the existing fabric.

12. Hot glue side and bottom edges of the wrong side of the frame front. Affix the frame front to the frame back, wrong sides together and edges aligned.

13. Hot glue the braid to all edges of the frame, wrapping it to the front and the back equally. Do not seal the opening in the top.

14. Hot glue the cord to the inside edge of the window.

15. Attach the stand.

Pansy Tray

MATERIALS
One dark wood frame with
   17½" x 10¼" window
Two medallion handles with screws
One 18" x 10¾" piece of ⅛"
   Masonite (to fit rabbet of frame)
Two 18" x 10¾" pieces of glass (to
   fit rabbet of frame)
Acrylic paint: purple, white
Paintbrush
Pressed dried pansies (enough for
   two layers)
Screwdriver
Nails
Hammer

DIRECTIONS
1. Center and attach the handles to
the short ends of the frame.

Frame a favorite thing—a funny photo, a greeting card, some dried flowers—and turn your frame into a tray by adding handles. Then, serving a drink to a friend will bring a smile to everyone's face.

2. Mix the purple paint with a small
amount of white paint and paint the
smooth side of the Masonite,
allowing some streaks to remain.
Allow to dry.

3. Arrange one layer of dried
pansies on the painted surface and
place one piece of glass over the
pansies.

4. Arrange a second layer of pansies on the glass and cover with the
second piece of glass.

5. Insert layers of Masonite, pansies, and glass in frame. Secure
with nails.

Horseshoe Frame

MATERIALS

Size #1 horseshoe
¾" x 5¼" x 7" weathered,
    distressed wood for center
14" of ¹⁄₁₆" x ³⁄₁₆" wood strip for
    molding inside window
14½" of ¹⁄₁₆" x ⅜" wood strip for
    molding around window
27" of ¼" x ¾" wood strips for
    molding
17" of ³⁄₁₆" x ¾" wood strips for
    outer molding
⅝" x 2" x 5½" wood piece for
    frame stand
½" x 2½" x 3½" wood piece for
    window back
Eighteen ¼" finishing nails
Nail set to fit heads of finishing nails
Wood filler
Eleven ½" wood screws
Hammer
Four upholstery tacks
Eight smooth brass round-headed
    tacks
Wood stain in desired color
Tracing paper
Pencil
Polyurethane coating
Paintbrush
Wood glue
Small clamps
Keyhole saw
Band saw
Sandpaper and/or belt sander
2½" x 3½" piece of acrylic or glass
Drill with ¼" bit

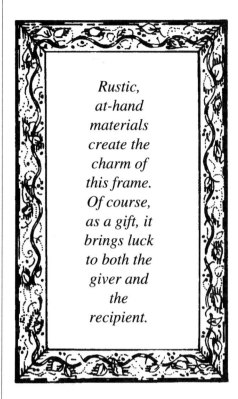

Rustic, at-hand materials create the charm of this frame. Of course, as a gift, it brings luck to both the giver and the recipient.

DIRECTIONS

Trim the Window

1. Using keyhole saw, cut 2½" x 3¼" window in center wood piece (Diagram 1).

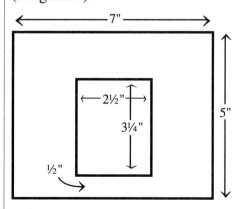

DIAGRAM 1

2. Measure and cut ¹⁄₁₆" x ³⁄₁₆" molding into four strips to fit inside the edges of the window, mitering the corners.

3. Using two finishing nails on each strip, nail the strips inside the window, placing edges flush with the front of the center piece (Diagram 2).

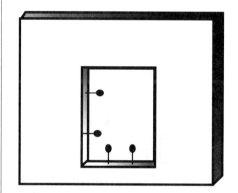

DIAGRAM 2

4. Cut four ¹⁄₁₆" x ⅜" strips to fit around the face of the window, mitering the corners (Diagram 3).

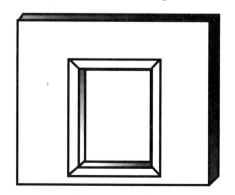

DIAGRAM 3

5. Place the center frame piece with window face up on a flat surface. Position the molding strips around the window and outline the edges to mark the position.

6. Place the horseshoe in position over the molding strips and mark the strips for trimming as needed at the corners (see photo).

7. Trim the corners of the molding.

8. Using sandpaper, round the edges of the molding strips.

9. Glue the strips with the trimmed corners around the window according to the marks.

10. Nail two finishing nails through each strip. Countersink nails. Fill holes with wood filler. Sand filler flush.

Trim the Outer Frame Edges

1. Cut ¼" x ¾" molding into two 7" strips and two 5½" strips.

2. Glue the 5½" pieces to the short edges of the center piece of wood and the 7" pieces to the long edges. Clamp and allow to set.

3. Sand these edge pieces flush with the front and back surfaces of the frame. Round molding edges and corners with belt sander or sandpaper.

4. Nail finishing nails into each strip of molding and into the frame. Countersink nails. Fill holes with wood filler. Sand filler flush.

5. Cut ³⁄₁₆" x ¾" molding into one 7" and two 5" pieces. Sand edges and round off ends.

6. Center and glue 7" piece to top of frame and 5" pieces on the short sides. Clamp and allow to set.

7. Drill three evenly-spaced starter holes about $^1/_{32}$" deep in each of these ³⁄₁₆" strips. Insert wood screws and screw until heads are slightly countersunk (Diagram 4).

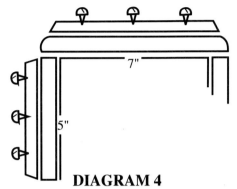

DIAGRAM 4

Make the Stand

1. Using tracing paper and a pencil, trace the stand pattern and cut it out.

2. Place the stand pattern on the ⅝" x 2" x 5½" wood piece and cut out one stand.

3. Drill two $1/32$"-deep starter holes according to the pattern.

Complete the Finishing Touches

1. Sand and stain the window back, stand, and frame as desired. Let dry.

2. Nail one upholstery tack in each corner of the frame front (see photo).

3. Apply one coat of polyurethane to all surfaces of the frame, including tacks and screw heads; allow to dry.

4. Place the horseshoe in position on the frame front. Secure with brass tacks through clinch holes in the shoe.

5. Place the frame face down on a flat surface. Insert acrylic or glass in the window. Insert photo. Glue the window back over the opening.

6. Glue the stand in place on the back of the frame, aligning lower edge. Clamp and allow to set.

7. Insert remaining two wood screws in the frame stand. Screw in place until heads are slightly countersunk.

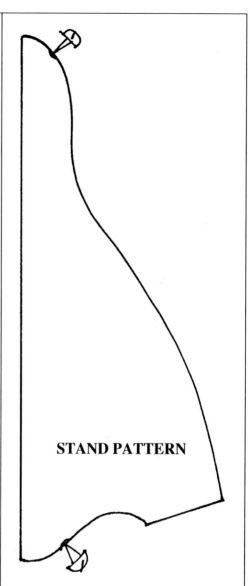

STAND PATTERN

Memory Box

MATERIALS

One frame with 10½" x 12½"
    window for lid
Molding, similar to but wider than
    frame molding (see Step 6)
Mat board: two 11" x 13" pieces
    and one piece large enough
    for Step 9
One 14" x 16 piece of melon moiré
    taffeta
Scissors
Ruler
Craft knife
2 yards of ¼" wide cream silk
    ribbon
Wood stain to match frame
Tacky glue
Hammer
Eight to twelve small nails
Staple gun and staples

DIRECTIONS

1. Center one piece of the 11" x 13" mat board on the wrong side of the taffeta. Wrap the taffeta to the wrong side of the mat board and glue the edges to the mat board. Trim any excess from the corners.

2. Place varied lengths of ribbon loosely across the front of the taffeta, cutting the ribbon as needed and anchoring each end of the ribbon to the back of the mat with glue.

Beautiful moldings join with beautiful memories and sentimental mementos to make this lasting keepsake.

3. Mount the taffeta in the frame.

4. Mount the second 11" x 13" mat board behind the first, recessed in the frame.

5. Measure the outside edges of the lid to determine the size for the box. Add a little to each side measurement to allow for mitered corners, depending on the shape of the molding. (The rabbet of the

molding must be slightly larger than the outside edges of the lid so the lid will sit in the rabbet of the side molding.)

6. Using these measurements and allowing for miters, cut the molding into four pieces of the correct length. Cut the molding so that the rabbet edge is upright and the front face of the molding is the side of the box. (Diagram 1).

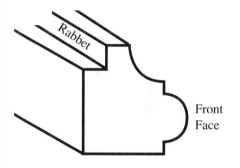

Rabbet

Front
Face

DIAGRAM 1

7. Glue and nail the molding to make the sides of the box.

8. Touch up the stain on the inside edges of the molding, if needed.

9. Cut the large mat board to fit the outside edges of the wider molding.

10. Staple this mat board to the bottom edges of the box sides.

Fabric Tray

MATERIALS

One embossed frame with
   15½" x 9½" window
Two handles with screws
Acrylic paints: orange, gold
Two 16" x 10" pieces of mat
   board (to fit rabbet of frame)
One 16" x 10" piece of glass (to
   fit rabbet of frame)
One 17" x 11" piece of fabric
About ½ yard of 1"-wide navy
   ribbon, or enough to wrap
   around the handles
Screwdriver
Small nails
Glue

DIRECTIONS

1. Prepare the frame for painting.

2. Paint an orange basecoat on the frame.

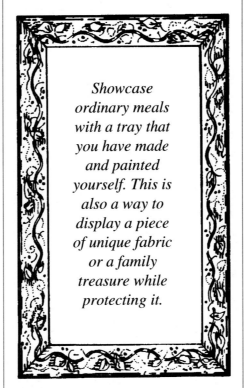

Showcase ordinary meals with a tray that you have made and painted yourself. This is also a way to display a piece of unique fabric or a family treasure while protecting it.

3. Paint the raised edges with gold; allow to dry.

4. Center and attach the handles to the short ends of the frame.

5. Cut the ribbon into two 9" pieces and wrap it in a spiral around the handles. Glue the ends in place.

6. Center one piece of the mat board on the wrong side of the fabric. Wrap the edges of the fabric to the back of the mat board and glue.

7. Insert the glass in the frame.

8. Insert the fabric-covered mat with the right side next to the glass.

9. Insert the second piece of mat board. Secure on back with small nails.

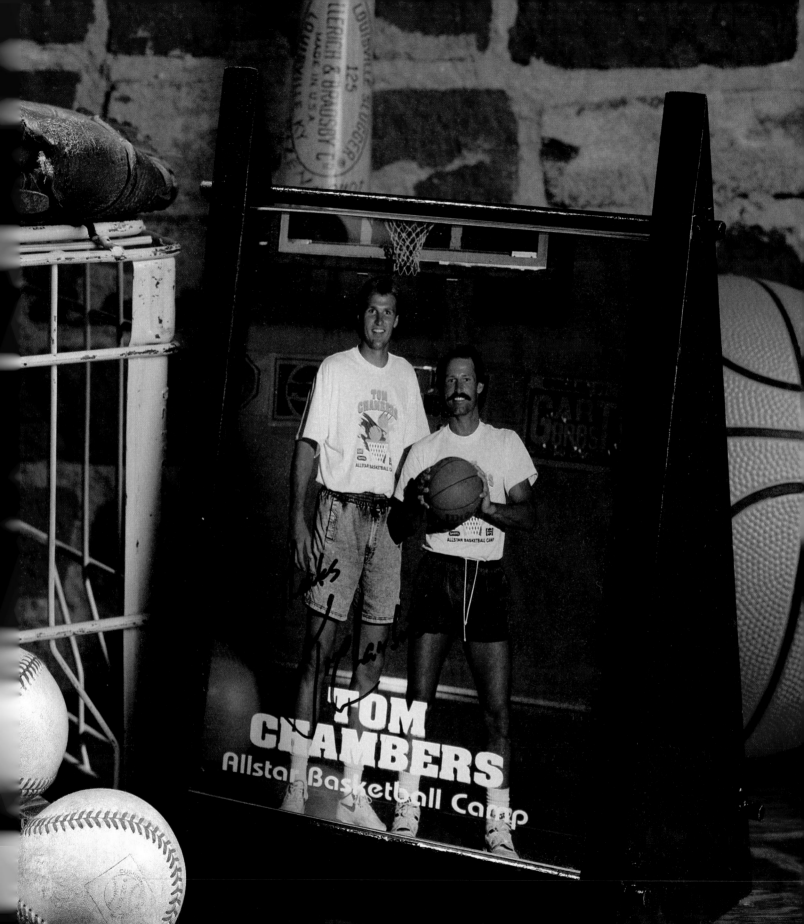

Stand Alone Triangles

MATERIALS

One 1" x 8" x 30" piece of pine
    board (rough mill measurement)
Paper
Pencil
Saw
Three ¼" dowels 10" long
Six round toothpicks
Two 8" x 10" pieces of ¹⁄₁₆" thick
    acrylic
Two 8" x 10" pieces of mat board
Router with ¼" bit
Oil-base enamel paint: dark blue
Drill with ¹⁄₁₆" and ⁵⁄₁₆" bits
Fine sandpaper
Ruler

DIRECTIONS

1. Using paper, a ruler and a pencil, draft and cut-out the frame pattern (see Diagram).

2. Place the pattern on the pine board, trace around the pattern, and cut out two pieces. Drill three ⁵⁄₁₆" holes in each frame piece and rout each piece (see Diagram).

3. Drill ¹⁄₁₆" holes about ⅜" from the end of each dowel.

4. Sand the frame and the dowels.

5. Paint all surfaces dark blue; allow to dry.

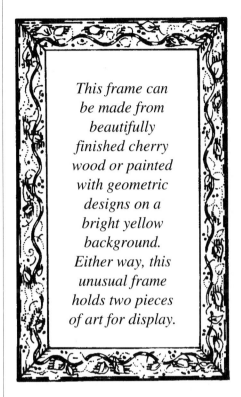

This frame can be made from beautifully finished cherry wood or painted with geometric designs on a bright yellow background. Either way, this unusual frame holds two pieces of art for display.

6. Insert two dowels through the bottom holes of one triangular frame piece.

7. To secure the dowels, cut ¾" pieces of toothpick and place them in the holes on the outside of the frame.

8. Sandwich art between one piece of mat board and one piece of acrylic. Repeat to make another mat board/art/acrylic sandwich.

9. Position these "sandwiches" with mat boards back-to-back and insert in rout.

10. Place the second frame piece against the edge of the "sandwiches" and attach by placing the two bottom dowels through the holes in the second frame piece. Secure with toothpicks.

11. Place the third dowel through the top holes of the triangular frame pieces and secure with toothpicks.

12. Paint the toothpicks dark blue; allow to dry.

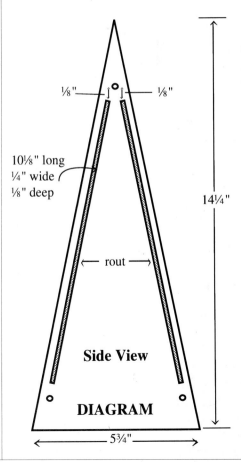

⅛"   ⅛"

10⅛" long
¼" wide
⅛" deep

← rout →

14¼"

Side View

DIAGRAM

← 5¾" →

It's Clearly Love

MATERIALS

Two 14" x 15" pieces of acrylic
½"-wide double-sided tape
One 10" x 10" or smaller die-cut
   greeting card
4½ yards of 1½"-wide pink wired
   ribbon
2¼ yards of 1"-wide cotton ecru flat
   lace
Fabric glue
Scissors
Hot glue gun and glue

DIRECTIONS

1. Center the greeting card face side up on one piece of acrylic. Apply a border of tape to the perimeter of the acrylic. Place the second piece of acrylic on top of the first, aligning all edges; press together to secure.

2. Apply a border of tape to the perimeter of the front piece of acrylic.

3. Cut a 60" long piece of the pink ribbon.

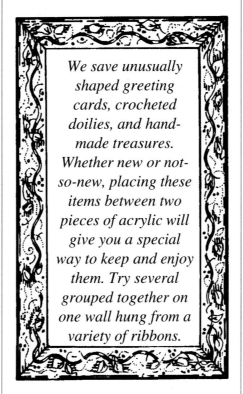

We save unusually shaped greeting cards, crocheted doilies, and hand-made treasures. Whether new or not-so-new, placing these items between two pieces of acrylic will give you a special way to keep and enjoy them. Try several grouped together on one wall hung from a variety of ribbons.

4. Apply the ribbon to the front acrylic piece, overlapping the ribbon to the edge of the tape (Diagram 1) and mitering corners (Diagram 2). Add small pieces of tape in the corners as needed.

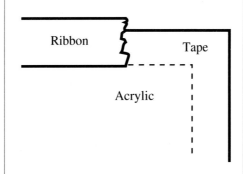

DIAGRAM 1

DIAGRAM 2

5. Place acrylic face down and apply a border of tape to back edges. Wrap the ribbon from front to back, mitering corners.

6. Using fabric glue, apply lace on top of the ribbon, again mitering the corners.

7. Cut the remaining pink ribbon into one 24" piece and two 40" pieces.

8. Mark the center of the 24"-piece of ribbon. Turn under and glue the raw ends. Then, glue ends to the upper back corners of the acrylic.

9. If desired, and handling the two 40"-pieces of ribbon as one, tie them into a large bow. Then, hot glue the bow to the center of the 24"-ribbon.

Be My Sunshine

MATERIALS

Mat board: three 8" x 8" pieces, one 5½" x 3½" piece
Compass
Pencil
Craft knife
Paintbrushes
Acrylic paints: black, gold, orange
3½ yards of 1½"-wide flat white picot lace
Needle and thread
3½" of ⅜"-wide white satin ribbon
Porcelainizing stiffener
Hot glue gun and glue

DIRECTIONS

1. Using a compass and a pencil, draw a 7"-diameter circle on each of the large mat boards. In one circle, draw a 3¾"-diameter circular window and in another, a 5½"-diameter circular window. Then, cut out all three circles. Use the 5½" x 3½" piece for the stand. (For directions on how to make the stand, see General Instructions, page 15.)

2. Paint the mat board with the smaller window black.

3. Paint the edges of the window on the other mat board black.

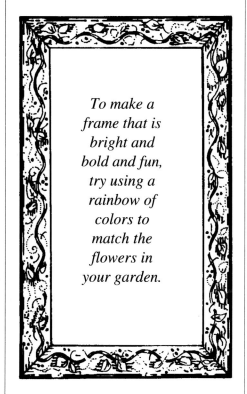

To make a frame that is bright and bold and fun, try using a rainbow of colors to match the flowers in your garden.

4. Cut the white picot lace into two pieces: one 1½ yards long; the other, 2 yards long.

5. Sew a gathering stitch along the straight edge of each piece of lace.

6. To make the back ruffle, gather the 2-yard piece to 20". Glue the edge of the lace to the front of the mat with the smaller window ¼" from the outside edge, distributing the fullness evenly.

7. To make the front ruffle, gather the 1½-yard piece to 16½". Glue the edge of the lace to the mat board with the larger window, extending the gathered edge slightly inside the window edge.

8. Using a paintbrush, apply stiffener to all of the lace, covering it thoroughly but without filling holes. Allow to dry overnight.

9. Paint all the lace with gold paint, adding orange for accent as desired.

10. Center and glue the sides and bottom of the back mat to the mat with the smaller window, leaving the top open for inserting the picture.

11. Center and glue all the edges of the mat with the large window on top of the mat with the small window.

12. Attach the stand.

Lace Frames

Sweet Memories
MATERIALS

Mat board: two 6" x 7½" pieces and one 4½" x 2¼" piece
¾ yard of 1½"-wide flat white trim
Porcelainizing stiffener
Paintbrush
½ yard of light blue ⅛"-wide silk ribbon
⅜ yard of pink ⅛"-wide silk ribbon
⅛ yard of light green ⅛"-wide silk ribbon
3½" of ⅜"-wide white satin ribbon
Tracing paper
Pencil
Craft knife
Hot glue gun and glue
Needle and thread
Tweezers

DIRECTIONS

1. Using tracing paper and a pencil, trace the heart pattern on page 66 and cut it out.

2. Place the heart pattern on one of the large pieces of mat board and cut out the outer edges of one heart (with no window) for the back of the frame. Then, place the pattern on the other large piece of mat board and cut out one heart with a heart-shaped window for the front of the frame. Use the 4½" x 2¼" piece for the stand. (For directions on how to make the stand, see General Instructions, page 15.)

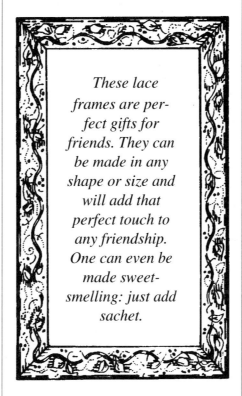

These lace frames are perfect gifts for friends. They can be made in any shape or size and will add that perfect touch to any friendship. One can even be made sweet-smelling: just add sachet.

3. Fold ½"-deep pleats in the straight edges of the white trim. Sew a running stitch along the edge to secure the pleats.

4. With the ends of the trim at the center top, glue the pleated edge to the window edge of the frame front.

5. Spray the trim with stiffener.

6. Tie the blue ribbon into a bow. Spray it with stiffener and attach it to the upper right lobe of the heart, twisting the ribbon tails slightly. (The stiffener will act as an adhesive.)

7. Cut three 3" pieces from the pink ribbon.

8. To make ribbon flowers, tie a knot at one end of one piece of pink ribbon. Ravel the raw end slightly. With tweezers, pull two threads from the center of the raw end and gather the ribbon tightly. Tack the raw end to the knot with a small amount of stiffener.

9. Repeat Step 8 to make three pink ribbon flowers.

10. Cut three 1" pieces from the green ribbon. Fold each piece into a small loop. Then, using tweezers to handle these green leaves and stiffener as an adhesive, attach the leaves to the center of the blue bow.

11. Again using tweezers and stiffener, attach the pink ribbon flowers to the bow and leaves.

12. Using a paintbrush, apply stiffener to all the trim and ribbons, covering thoroughly but without filling holes. Allow to dry overnight.

13. Attach the stand.

Cutting line for front

Cutting line for back and front

**LACE FRAME
HEART PATTERN**

Sachet Frame
MATERIALS

Mat board: two 6" x 6" pieces and
   one 2" x 3½" piece
10" x 10" piece of bridal net
Compass
Pencil
Craft knife
½ cup of potpourri
Small plate
Glue
Adhesive spray
1¼ yard of batiste eyelet
Seven dried rosebuds
⅜ yard of ⅛"-wide silk ribbon:
   pink, white, burgundy
3" of ⅜"-wide white satin ribbon

DIRECTIONS

1. Using a pencil and a compass, draw one 5"-diameter circle for the back and one 5"-diameter circle with a 3"-diameter window for the front on the two large pieces of mat board. Then, cut out the two circles. Use the 2" x 3½" piece for the stand. (For directions on how to make the stand, see General Instructions, page 15.)

2. Again, using a compass and a pencil, draw a 8"-diameter circle with a 2"-diameter window on the bridal net and cut it out on both lines.

3. Place the front mat over the bridal net and mark the window edge on the net. Cut tabs in the bridal net from the cut-out window edge nearly to the marked edge.

4. Pour potpourri onto a small plate. Spray adhesive on the right side of the mat. Dip mat into the potpourri. Repeat as needed to build up potpourri on the mat.

5. Place the mat with potpourri side up on a flat surface and place the bridal net over the potpourri. Carefully turn the mat and net until face down. Then, fold the net tabs to the inside and glue them to the back of the mat.

6. Gently fold the outside edges of the net to the back and glue.

7. Gather the edge of the eyelet to 15½". Glue this gathered edge to the back of the mat.

8. Handling all three ribbon lengths as one, tie them into a loose bow.

9. Glue the bow to the center top of the mat. Then, glue the rosebuds over the knot.

10. Using spray adhesive, mount art to back mat.

11. Hot glue the back mat to the front mat.

12. Attach the stand.

Glass on Glass

MATERIALS

One 8" x 10" mat with oval window
Mat board: one 8" x 10" piece and
    one 8½" x 5½" piece (for the
    stand)
Craft knife
Wrapping paper
Spray adhesive
Double-sided tape
Hot glue gun and glue
Two 8" x 10" pieces of glass
¾ yard of 1/16"-wide gold cord
1⅛ yards of 1⅞"-wide gold braid
    with decorative edge

DIRECTIONS

Make the Mat and Frame

1. Cut two 8" x 10" pieces from the wrapping paper.

2. Spray adhesive on the mat with the oval window and on the 8" x 10" mat. Attach the wrong side of an 8" x 10" piece of wrapping paper to each piece of mat board.

3. Cut the wrapping paper ½" inside and all the way around the oval window. Cut perpendicular lines nearly to the edge of the window. Fold the tabs to the back of the mat and glue.

4. Mount the art between the mats. Secure.

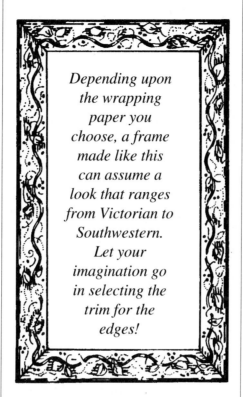

Depending upon the wrapping paper you choose, a frame made like this can assume a look that ranges from Victorian to Southwestern. Let your imagination go in selecting the trim for the edges!

5. Attach tape to all the edges of the mat with the oval window. Place the mats wrong sides together, edges aligned, and press to secure.

6. Hot glue the outside edge of one piece of glass to the mat front. Repeat for the back. (With the mats between two layers of glass, the frame looks finished and attractive from the back as well as from the front.)

7. Glue the gold cord around the oval window (see photo). Set aside remaining cord.

8. Glue the gold braid with decorative edge around the frame, centering it over the edges of the glass and mats with the decorative edge overlapping the wrapping paper. Wrap the trim to the front and back and glue as needed.

Make and Decorate the Stand

1. Use the 8½" x 5½" piece of mat board for the stand. (For directions on how to make the stand, see General Instructions, page 15.)

2. Cut one piece wrapping paper the same size as the stand piece and one piece like the stand piece but with ½" added to all edges.

3. To cover the stand, place the wrapping paper with ½" margin wrong side up. Spray adhesive on one side of the mat stand. Center the stand on the wrapping paper, folding the margins to the back side and trimming any excess from the corners. Glue.

4. Spray adhesive on the wrong side of the other piece of wrapping paper. Center it over the mat stand.

5. Attach the stand, using remaining gold cord in place of ribbon.

Clay Magnet Frames

MATERIALS
Polymer clay: red, green, black, white, blue, yellow
Acrylic paints: red, dark red
Paintbrushes
Glossy clear resin spray
Adhesive-backed magnetic sheet
Tracing paper
Pencil
Craft knife
Rolling pin
Scissors
Tacky glue

Note: Polymer clays are available in a wide variety of colors. We used six different colors of clay, but if you want to use fewer, you can paint the clay after baking and prior to coating with resin spray. Use a craft knife to cut clay.

DIRECTIONS
Watermelon Frame
1. Using tracing paper and a pencil, trace the watermelon frame patterns on page 72 and cut them out.

2. Roll out white, red, and green clay to ¼" thickness.

3. Place the watermelon frame pattern on the white clay and cut out the frame.

4. Place the melon pattern on the red clay and cut out four melons.

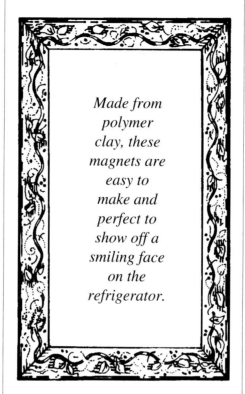

Made from polymer clay, these magnets are easy to make and perfect to show off a smiling face on the refrigerator.

5. Cut four thin strips from green clay and press along curved edge of melons to make rinds.

6. Make 12 tiny black clay balls and flatten to make seeds.

Star Frame
1. Using tracing paper and a pencil, trace the star frame patterns on page 72 and cut them out.

2. Roll out blue and yellow clay to ¼" thickness.

3. Place the circular frame pattern on the blue clay and cut it out.

4. Place the star pattern on the yellow clay and cut out three stars.

5. Place the moon pattern on the yellow clay and cut out one moon.

Wreath Frame
1. Note: Bow is painted on. Using tracing paper and a pencil, trace the wreath pattern on page 72 and cut it out.

2. Roll out the green clay to ¼" thickness.

3. Place the wreath pattern on the green clay and cut out one wreath.

4. Make fifteen ⅛" berries from red clay.

All Frames
1. Work the edges of each clay piece with your hands to make them smooth.

2. Position the pieces on each frame (see photo and patterns).

3. Bake the clay according to the manufacturer's directions.

4. Spray the frame fronts with resin; allow to dry.

5. Paint the bow on the wreath red. Then, shade with darker red.

6. Cut magnetic sheet to match the shapes of the three frames.

7. Cut photos ⅛" to ¼" smaller than the magnetic sheets.

8. Remove the protective sheet on each magnet and place the photo on the magnet.

9. Place the magnet on the back of the frame and glue in place.

STAR FRAME PATTERNS

WATERMELON FRAME PATTERNS

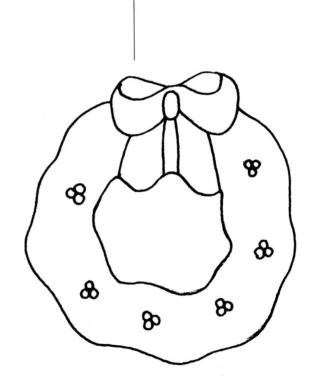

WREATH FRAME PATTERN

Cloud Screen Frame

Cloud Screen Frame

MATERIALS

One ½" x 8" x 40" planed pineboard
Tape
Craft knife
Jigsaw
Fine sandpaper
Two paintbrushes
Acrylic paint: light blue, white
Four 1½" bronze hinges
Screwdriver
One frame with 3½" x 5" window
One 3½" x 5" piece of gray mat
    board with 2" x 3" window
One 3" x 5" piece of floral print mat
    board
Glue

DIRECTIONS

Make the Screen

1. Enlarge the patterns for the screen on page 75. Follow the directions with the grid or enlarge the patterns using a photocopying machine (Diagram 1).

2. Tape the patterns to the pine board, and then, using a jigsaw, cut out one of each panel.

3. Using fine sandpaper, sand the panels to prepare them for painting.

4. Paint a light blue basecoat on all surfaces. Allow to dry.

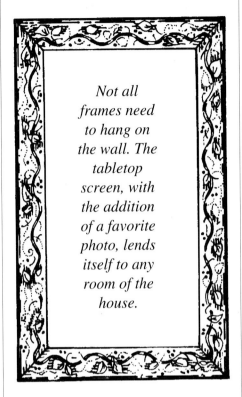

Not all frames need to hang on the wall. The tabletop screen, with the addition of a favorite photo, lends itself to any room of the house.

5. Add water to the white paint, diluting it until it is the consistency of ink. Then, cover all surfaces of the panels with a thin wash of white. Allow to dry.

6. Attach the hinges (Diagram 2), making sure that both end panels fold forward.

DIAGRAM 1

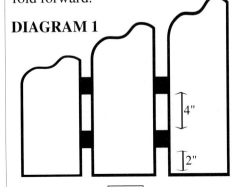

4"

2"

Make the Mat

1. Cut the floral print mat board into four pieces: two 3½" x ½" pieces and two 4" x ½" pieces.

2. Glue the floral mat pieces to the gray mat, leaving a ¼" border of gray mat around the window (Diagram 3).

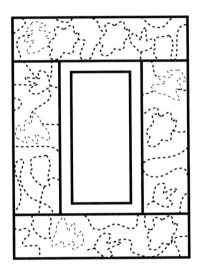

DIAGRAM 3

3. Glue the frame to the floral mat.

4. Mount the art. Secure.

5. Glue the frame to the screen (see photo).

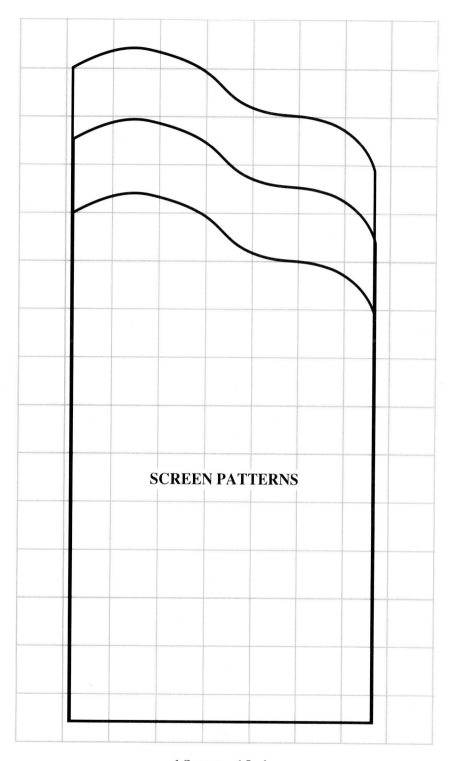

SCREEN PATTERNS

1 Square = 1 Inch

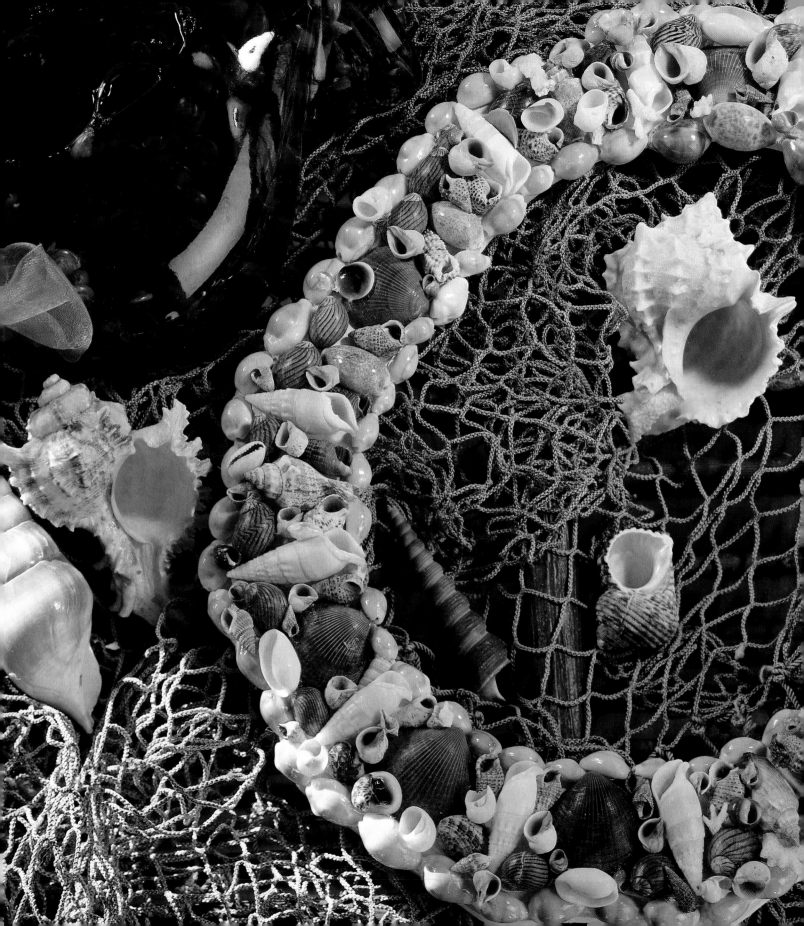

Oval Shell Frame

MATERIALS
One 12" x 14" oval wood frame
Acrylic paint: ivory
Paintbrush
Hot glue gun and glue
Eight 2"-wide scallop shells
Twelve 1½"-long spiral shells
Collection of shells of same size
   and shape
Assorted small shells

DIRECTIONS
1. Prepare the frame for painting.

2. Paint the frame with two coats of ivory. Allow to dry.

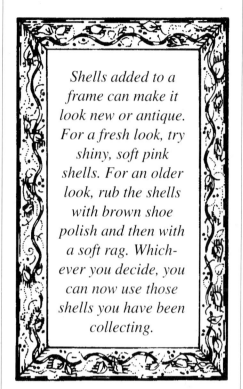

Shells added to a frame can make it look new or antique. For a fresh look, try shiny, soft pink shells. For an older look, rub the shells with brown shoe polish and then with a soft rag. Whichever you decide, you can now use those shells you have been collecting.

3. Hot glue scallop and spiral shells at even intervals (Diagram 1).

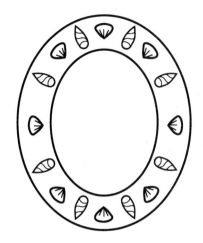

DIAGRAM 1

4. Hot glue shells of the same size and shape along the inside and outside edges of the frame.

5. Using an assortment of small shells, fill in remaining spaces, overlapping shells as desired.

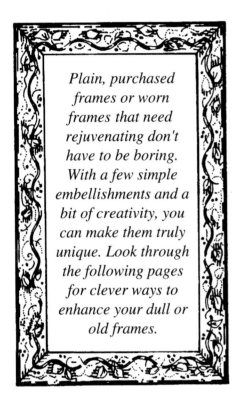

Plain, purchased frames or worn frames that need rejuvenating don't have to be boring. With a few simple embellishments and a bit of creativity, you can make them truly unique. Look through the following pages for clever ways to enhance your dull or old frames.

Chapter Two

Beachcomber Treasure

MATERIALS

One ready-made frame with
   2½" to 3"-wide weathered
   barnwood molding
Acrylic paints: blue-gray, white
Paintbrushes
Assorted seashells
Tacky glue
Scrap paper
Toothbrush

DIRECTIONS

1. Prepare the frame for painting.

2. Paint the frame blue-gray; allow to dry. (The photo shows a frame with an inner panel that has been painted white, then lightly washed with blue-gray.)

3. Arrange the shells in a group at the bottom of the frame (see photo).

A frame can take on an entirely new look when objects are added. Use your imagination and consider old pieces of jewelry, a collection of antique buttons, or a variety of beads saved through the years.

4. Glue the shells to the frame using a large amount of glue and allowing it to build up between shells. Allow to dry overnight.

5. Paint the glue and edges of the shells blue-gray. Wipe the shells to remove most of the paint while it is still wet.

6. Cover the shells loosely with paper.

7. Splatter paint the entire frame with white paint, allowing small blobs to remain. To splatter paint, dip the toothbrush into the paint and, holding the toothbrush 3" to 6" from the frame, draw your finger across the brush, allowing the paint to splatter onto the frame.

8. Clean any splatters from the surfaces of the shells. Allow to dry.

Vinegar Painted Frames

Green Frame
MATERIALS

One unfinished wood frame
Acrylic paint: gold
1"- or ¾"-wide flat paintbrush
2 tablespoons of vinegar
1 teaspoon of sugar
Watercolor pigment in tube: green
Polymer clay
Spray gloss varnish

DIRECTIONS

1. Prepare the frame for painting.

2. Paint the frame gold; allow to dry.

3. Mix vinegar and sugar with one drop of green watercolor pigment; adjust color as desired.

4. Use the mixture to paint over the entire surface of the frame. Allow to sit one minute. Then, dry brush the surface again to spread the paint mixture evenly. (The vinegar paint will be sticky; avoid fingerprints.)

5. Mold a leaf shape, about ½" long, from the clay.

6. While the paint on the frame is still wet, use the clay leaf as a stamp and stamp randomly on the surface of the vinegar paint (see photo).

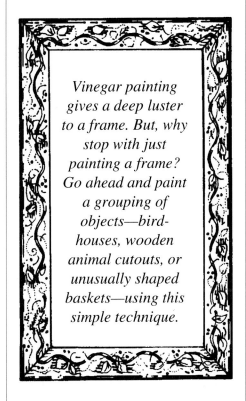

Vinegar painting gives a deep luster to a frame. But, why stop with just painting a frame? Go ahead and paint a grouping of objects—birdhouses, wooden animal cutouts, or unusually shaped baskets—using this simple technique.

7. Using the end of the paintbrush handle, make stems on the leaves. Allow to dry two to three hours. (The surface may seem wet because it remains sticky.)

8. Spray with two or three coats of varnish.

Blue Frame
MATERIALS

One frame
Acrylic paints: turquoise, lavender, purple
Paintbrushes: one 1"- or ¾"-wide flat brush and one round
2 tablespoons of vinegar
1 teaspoon of sugar
Watercolor pigment in tube: blue
Glossy varnish

DIRECTIONS

1. Prepare the frame for painting.

2. Using a flat brush, paint the frame turquoise. Allow to dry.

3. Mix vinegar and sugar with one drop of blue watercolor pigment; adjust color as desired.

4. Use the mixture to paint over the entire surface of the frame. Allow to sit one minute. Then, dry brush the surface again to spread the paint mixture evenly. (The vinegar paint will be sticky; avoid fingerprints.)

5. To make the pattern, twirl the round brush in rows in the wet vinegar mixture on the frame (see photo). Allow to dry.

6. Using the flat brush, paint the window edges purple and the outside edges of the frame lavender.

7. Spray with two or three coats of varnish.

Farmhouse-Fresh Frames

Milk Paint Frame
MATERIALS
One unfinished wood frame
Milk paint in desired color
Paintbrushes
Spray matte varnish

DIRECTIONS
1. Mix the milk paint according to the manufacturer's directions.

2. Paint the frame; allow to dry.

3. Brush excess dry paint from the surface of the frame.

4. Spray with two coats of varnish.

Inexpensive, raw wood frames can take on a very appealing country look if you stain them with a simple wash of color. One easy way to get a fresh look is to dye a wood frame to match other pieces in the room; another way is to use milk paint, which gives a chalky look.

Dyed Frame
MATERIALS
One unfinished wood frame
One package of fabric dye in
    desired color
Newspapers
Spray mat varnish

DIRECTIONS
1. Fill the sink with enough hot water to immerse the frame. Add a package of dye and stir to dissolve.

2. Place the frame in the dye for 5-10 minutes.

3. Remove the frame and place it on newspapers to dry.

4. Spray with two coats of varnish.

Gold Leaf Frame

MATERIALS

One frame with flat molding
Five small wooden flower cutouts
Wood glue
Acrylic paint: yellow gold
Paintbrush: soft-bristled for gold
    leafing, flat for acrylic paint
Gold leafing sheets
Gold leafing spray adhesive
Spray varnish

DIRECTIONS

1. Prepare the frame for painting.

2. Glue the flower cutouts in an arch across the top of the frame (see photo).

3. Using the flat brush, apply the yellow gold paint; allow to dry.

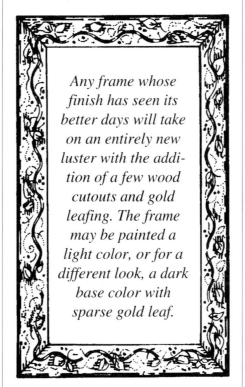

Any frame whose finish has seen its better days will take on an entirely new luster with the addition of a few wood cutouts and gold leafing. The frame may be painted a light color, or for a different look, a dark base color with sparse gold leaf.

4. Spray the frame with gold leafing adhesive, carefully coating all surfaces, including the edges, that are to be coated with gold leaf.

5. Gently place the gold leaf sheets on the frame surface. Smooth using the dry soft brush.

6. Reapply additional gold leaf sheets, if needed, to cover any gaps. (Layers of gold leafing add to the interest of the frame.)

7. Brush away excess.

8. Seal with two coats of spray varnish.

Pastel Marbleized Frames

Multi-Colored Marbleized Frame

MATERIALS

One embossed plaster frame with
   4" x 4¾" window
Paintbrushes: one fine tip, one flat
Acrylic paints: pink, light green,
   yellow, lavender, dark green
Sponges
Spray gloss varnish

DIRECTIONS

1. Prepare the frame for painting.

2. Paint the frame pink.

3. Using sponges, apply the following colors in sequence, allowing the basecoat to show through: light green, yellow, lavender, dark green.

4. Using the fine-tipped brush and dark green paint, brush on veins and accent dots. Allow to dry.

5. Apply two or three coats of varnish.

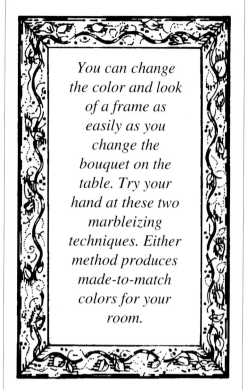

You can change the color and look of a frame as easily as you change the bouquet on the table. Try your hand at these two marbleizing techniques. Either method produces made-to-match colors for your room.

Mauve Marbleized Frame

MATERIALS

One embossed plaster frame with
   4" x 4¾" window
Acrylic paint: mauve
Paintbrush
Oil-based enamel spray paint:
   cream
Shallow pan larger than frame
Spray gloss varnish

DIRECTIONS

1. Prepare the frame for painting.

2. Paint the frame mauve, applying two coats, if needed. Allow to dry.

3. Fill the pan with ¾" of water.

4. Spray the cream paint over the surface of the water, covering an area about the size of the frame. (The paint will float in a thin layer on the surface of the water.)

5. Holding the front of the frame down and parallel with the surface of the water, quickly dip the front of the frame into the paint on the water deep enough to coat the surface.

6. Turn the frame right side up and allow to dry.

Birds and Boughs

Birds and Boughs

MATERIALS

One frame with 15½" x 19½"
   window with 3½"-wide molding
   (with mirror)
One ⅜" x 3" x 36" piece of balsa
   wood
Tracing paper
Pencil
Graphite paper
Small sharp knife
Craft knife
Sponge
Acrylic paints: dark green, blue-
   green, avocado green, medium
   green, yellow, red, tan, black
Paintbrushes
One 24" branch ¾" thick
One 24" branch ¼" thick
One 7" branch with fork
Wood glue
Two yards of 24-gauge copper wire
Wire cutters
Drill with ¹⁄₁₆" bit
Hot glue gun and glue

DIRECTIONS

Paint the Frame
1. Prepare the frame for painting.

2. Paint the entire frame dark green.

Make and Paint the Birds
1. Using tracing paper and a pencil,
trace the patterns for the bird and
the wing on page 97.

*Bring a bit of the
outdoors into
your home with
this cheerful trio
of birds. Secure a
mirror in any
sized frame with
two or three
turnbuttons on
each edge. The
branches are as
close as your
yard or a florist.*

2. Place the patterns on top of
graphite paper on top of the balsa
wood and retrace the patterns. (The
graphite paper will transfer the
designs to the balsa wood.) Using a
knife, cut out three birds and six
wings.

3. Bevel one edge of each wing to
about 45 degrees and fit the wings
to the birds as desired. Then, hot
glue the wings to the bird bodies.

4. Paint two birds yellow with tan
beaks and black eyes; allow to dry.

5. Paint the third bird red with a tan
beak and black eyes; allow to dry.

Make and Paint the Leaves
1. Using tracing paper and a pencil,
trace the two leaf patterns and cut
them out.

2. Place the large leaf pattern on top
of graphite paper on top of the balsa
wood and retrace it six times. Then,
cut out the six leaves.

3. Paint five of these large leaves
dark green and one avocado green.

4. Place the other leaf pattern on the
sponge and cut the sponge away
from the pattern to make a leaf
stamp.

5. Place the sponge leaf in paint and
sponge paint the small leaf shape
onto the face of the frame in a
random, overlapping pattern,
allowing the basecoat to show
through. Use blue-green, avocado
green, and medium green for these
sponge-painted leaves.

6. Freehand paint veins on the balsa
wood and sponge-painted leaves,
using all green paints as desired.

Complete the Finishing Touches
1. Position the branches on the
frame as desired.

2. Where branches touch the front
of the frame, drill two holes ½"

apart in the frame as needed, and use copper wire to secure the branches to the frame. Place the branch with the fork last over the top of the other branches.

3. Drill a hole in one end of each balsa leaf.

4. Using the copper wire, attach the balsa leaves to the branches (see photo.)

5. Hot glue the birds to the branches.

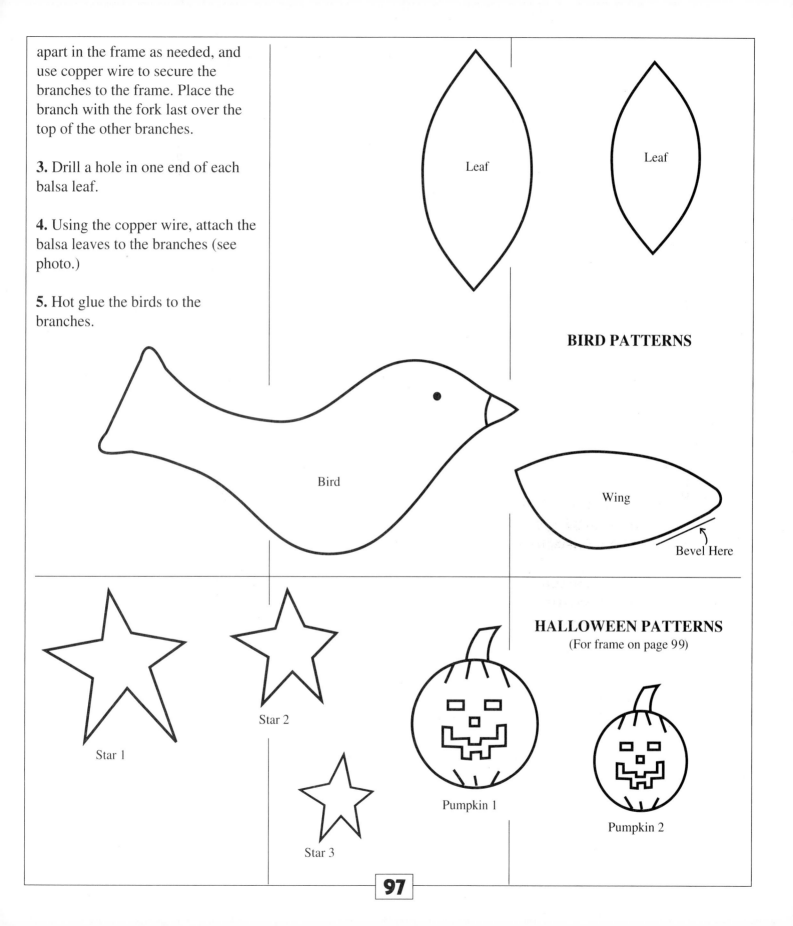

Leaf

Leaf

BIRD PATTERNS

Bird

Wing

Bevel Here

HALLOWEEN PATTERNS
(For frame on page 99)

Star 1

Star 2

Star 3

Pumpkin 1

Pumpkin 2

Halloween Frame

MATERIALS

One wood frame with 7" x 7" window and 2½"-wide flat molding
Spray paint: black acrylic, gold metallic
Two pounds of polymer clay
One cookie sheet
One rolling pin
Modeling tools: match stick, nail
Craft knife
Tracing paper
Pencil
Scissors
Acrylic paints: green, orange, blue, white
Paintbrushes
Wood glue
Semi-gloss spray varnish

DIRECTIONS

1. Prepare the frame for painting.

2. Spray the frame with black spray paint.

3. On the back side of a cookie sheet, shape the clay into a frame shape (Diagram 1).

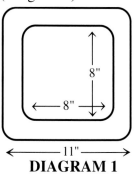

DIAGRAM 1

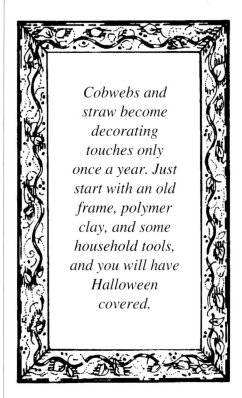

Cobwebs and straw become decorating touches only once a year. Just start with an old frame, polymer clay, and some household tools, and you will have Halloween covered.

4. Using a rolling pin, flatten the clay frame to about ¼"; it should be a little bigger than your frame.

5. Using modeling tools, add surface texture to the clay to make it resemble straw (see photo).

6. Using a craft knife, cut the outside edge of the clay frame, cutting in such a way that small sections of the clay will extend beyond the outside edges of the frame (see photo).

7. Using tracing paper and a pencil, trace the three star patterns on page 97. Then, cut them out.

8. Roll out some of the remaining clay to ¼" thick. Place the star patterns on the clay, and cut out one of star pattern 1, two of star pattern 2, and three of star pattern 3.

9. Add the stars to the clay straw (see photo).

10. Mold remaining clay into one 1" ball and two ½" balls. Flatten each ball to about ½" thick and incise with features shown on pumpkin patterns 1 and 2 on page 97.

11. Apply the pumpkins to the straw clay. Add more small pumpkins as desired (see photo).

12. Bake the clay according to manufacturer's directions. Allow to cool completely.

13. Spray the clay black. Add blue and white highlights to the top third of the clay frame and orange and green highlights to the lower two-thirds.

14. Dust the entire clay design with gold spray paint; allow to dry.

15. Using liberal amounts of wood glue, attach the clay design to the face of the frame.

16. Spray with two or three coats of varnish.

Mottled Green Ripples

MATERIALS
One wood frame
Acrylic paints: navy, purple, black,
    pearlescent white, iridescent
    green
Paintbrushes
Several sponges
Spray semi-gloss varnish

DIRECTIONS
1. Prepare the frame for painting.

2. Paint a navy basecoat on the frame.

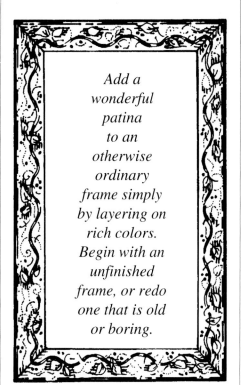

Add a wonderful patina to an otherwise ordinary frame simply by layering on rich colors. Begin with an unfinished frame, or redo one that is old or boring.

3. Using assorted brushes and paints, apply other colors using both wet brush and dry brush techniques. To wet brush, apply paint over wet paint and allow the colors to mix somewhat. To dry brush, use very small amounts of paint and skim it lightly over a dry surface, allowing underlying color to show through.

4. Apply paint using sponges; keep adding layers of paint—use green last—to get a mottled look. Allow to dry.

5. Apply two or three coats of varnish.

Quilt Lover's Frame

MATERIALS

One frame with 1¾"-wide molding
    and 9" x 12" window
Paintbrushes: one flat, one fine-
    tipped
Acrylic paints to match art
Coarse sandpaper
Tracing paper
Pencil
Scissors
Two artgum erasers
Craft knife
Spray mat varnish

DIRECTIONS

1. Prepare the frame for painting.

2. Using the flat brush, apply one coat of paint to the frame; allow to dry.

3. Sand lightly—just enough to slightly distress the finish.

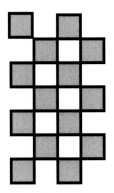

For this frame, we have used quilt motifs. You may prefer flowers or fish or fantasy creatures. Match your imagination to the art to be framed and then repeat the shapes and colors on the frame itself.

4. Paint an irregular pattern of small rectangles on the front and the sides of the frame in a slightly contrasting color (see light gold rectangles in photo).

5. Using tracing paper and a pencil, trace the patterns below. Then, cut them out.

6. Place the patterns on opposite sides of the two erasers, positioning them so that they are not directly behind each other.

7. Using the craft knife, cut the eraser away from the outside edges of the patterns to make raised stamps. Incise along any dotted lines shown on the patterns, leaving unmarked areas raised. Be sure that in cutting one side you do not cut into the pattern on the other side of the eraser.

8. Dip the eraser stamps in paint and use them to decorate the frame. Stamp the patterns at random on the frame in whatever colors you wish.

9. Spray the frame with two or three coats of varnish.

Very Flossy Frame

MATERIALS

One 7¼" x 8⅝" flat frame with
    4⅝" x 3¼" window
48" of ⅜"-wide dowels
One skein each of DMC embroidery
    floss: 817, 349, 350, 351, 352,
    353, 754, 948
Acrylic paints: pink, white
Paintbrush
Sponge
Spray gloss varnish
Ruler
Pencil
Scissors
Tacky glue

DIRECTIONS

1. Prepare the frame for painting.

2. Paint the frame pink. Then,
lightly sponge paint it with white.
Allow to dry.

3. Spray the painted frame with two
or three coats of varnish.

4. Cut the dowels into the following
pieces: two 8", two 8⅝", two 2½",
and two 4⅝". The dowels should fit
loosely around the frame and
window allowing for a layer of floss
in the corners.

Needleworkers are blessed with an astonishing array of embroidery floss colors from which to choose. We take advantage of this glorious palette to adorn a classic frame. You can use the palette shown or choose one to suit your decor.

5. Using a ruler, draw a pencil line
down the length of each dowel; this
line becomes the center back of the
dowel.

6. Arrange the floss skeins from
light to dark colors.

7. To wrap the floss, place a 1" tail
of the darkest (or lightest) color
floss on the pencil line on the dowel
and then wrap the floss over it and
around the dowel for about ½"
(Diagram 1). Bring the floss to the
back, cut, and using glue, tack the
end on the pencil line. Begin the
second color, wrap about ½", cut,
and glue. Continue with about ½"
of each color in order until the
dowel is completely wrapped.

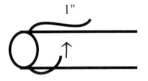

DIAGRAM 1

8. Planning the work so that the
dowels will be placed clockwise
around the frame, wrap the other
dowels, starting each dowel with
the next color in the sequence so
that the corners blend (see photo).

9. Glue the dowels to the edges of
the frame and window.

'Rain Dance'

Hundred Shades of Black

MATERIALS

One frame
Enamel paint: black
Paintbrush
Shallow pan larger than frame
Oil-based enamel spray paint: peach

DIRECTIONS

1. Prepare the frame for painting.

2. Paint the frame black, applying two coats, if needed. Allow to dry.

3. Fill the pan with ¾" of water.

4. Spray peach paint over the surface of the water in an area the size of the frame. (The paint will float in a thin layer on the surface of the water.)

The patterns produced with this technique are as unpredictable as the weather and will inspire just as much conversation! Begin with any new or used frame that will take paint—the wider the molding, the more impressive the results will be.

5. Holding the frame front down and parallel to the surface of the water, quickly dip the frame front into the paint on the water deep enough to coat the surface.

6. Turn the frame right side up; allow to dry.

Golden Notes

MATERIALS
One unfinished wood frame
Acrylic paints; purple, blue, black,
    metallic gold
Paintbrush
Small square of sponge
Spray semi-gloss varnish

DIRECTIONS
1. Prepare the frame for painting.

2. Mix purple, blue, and black paints to obtain an eggplant color.

3. Paint the frame with a base coat of this eggplant mixture.

Some inventive work with acrylic paints and a sponge makes an ordinary frame "sing" with rich embellishment.

4. Dip wet sponge into the gold paint and paint design (e.g., small blocks or musical notes) at random on the frame, wrapping any design made around the edges of the frame (see photo).

5. Dip the edge of the sponge in paint and fill in with straight lines where needed on designs.

6. Apply two coats of varnish.

Marbleized Floating Colors

MATERIALS

One wood frame
Large, shallow pan at least 1" larger
    on all sides than the frame
Newspapers
One gallon of liquid starch
Large plastic trash bag
Acrylic paints: light blue, bright
    blue, metallic gold
Three plastic cups (one for each
    color)
Three eyedroppers (one for each
    color)
Spoon
Design tool: comb, nail, or pencil

DIRECTIONS

1. Prepare the frame for painting.

2. Cut or tear one or two sections of newspaper into strips about 2" wide and as long as the marbleizing pan is wide.

3. Spread the remaining newspaper over the work surface.

4. Pour the liquid starch into the pan to 3" deep.

This method of marbleizing calls only for familiar household products and works well for marbleizing many frames at one time. The wonder of this method is that each finished piece will be unique. Experiment with different patterns and enjoy the various effects.

5. Use the strips of newspaper to skim the starch to remove surface tension.

6. Pour about 2 tablespoons of water to each cup, add drops of one color paint to each, and mix, diluting as necessary to obtain the consistency of whole milk.

7. Fill an eyedropper with one color of mixed paint. Hold the eyedropper just above the surface of the starch and gently float several drops of paint. The paint should spread into a thin, 3" to 4" circle. Some paint will sink to the bottom. (If all the paint sinks to the bottom, dilute the paint mixtures in the cups more.)

8. Repeat Step 7 with the two other colors, floating new colors on top of the first color or in a random pattern.

9. Use a design tool to guide the paint on the starch surface to form a pattern.

10. Hold the face of the frame down and parallel to the surface of the starch and immerse the frame, keeping it level.

11. After a few minutes, lift the frame, turn it right side up, and place it on a plastic bag to dry.

12. Use newspaper strips to skim the surface of the starch and remove left-over paint. (Different paints can then be added to the starch and other objects marbleized.)

Triple Features

Each of these frames is made from three separate frames that nest snugly together. The small frame fits inside the rabbet of the medium-size frame, and the medium frame fits inside the rabbet of the large frame. To ensure fit, the frames must be custom made. Then, round up your paints and brushes and try these treatments.

Triple Features

Heart Frame
MATERIALS

Three custom-made frames that nest together; the inner one should have a 6½" x 7½" window (Diagram, page 115)
Tracing paper
Graphite paper
Pencil
Ruler
Paintbrushes
Acrylic paints: burgundy, white, pink, dark pink
Glue
Nails
Hammer

DIRECTIONS

1. Prepare the three frames for painting.

2. Paint the largest frame burgundy; allow to dry.

3. Paint the medium frame white; allow to dry.

4. Paint the smallest frame pink; allow to dry.

5. Measure and mark even intervals for placing the hearts on the smallest frame.

6. Using tracing paper and a pencil, trace the heart pattern on page 115.

7. Refer to the photo and place the traced pattern on top of graphite paper on the smallest frame and retrace the design. (The graphite paper will transfer the design to the frame.)

8. Paint the hearts dark pink; allow to dry.

9. Fit the frames inside one another. Use glue and/or nails to attach them.

Star Frame
MATERIALS

Three custom-made frames that nest together; the inner one should have a 6½" x 7½" window (Diagram, page 115)
Tracing paper
Graphite paper
Pencil
Ruler
Paintbrushes
Acrylic paints: red, white, blue
Glue
Nails
Hammer

DIRECTIONS

1. Prepare the frames for painting.

2. Paint the largest frame red; allow to dry.

3. Paint the medium frame white; allow to dry.

4. Paint the smallest frame blue; allow to dry.

5. Measure and mark even intervals for placing the stars on the smallest frame.

6. Using tracing paper and a pencil, trace the star pattern on page 115.

7. Refer to the photo and place the traced pattern on top of graphite paper on the smallest frame and retrace the design. (The graphite paper will transfer the design to the frame.)

8. Paint the stars white; allow to dry.

9. Fit the frames inside one another. Use glue and/or nails to attach them.

Tree Frame

MATERIALS

Three custom-made frames that nest
    together; the inner one should
    have a 6½" x 7½" frame
    (Diagram)
Tracing paper
Graphite paper
Pencil
Ruler
Paintbrushes
Acrylic paints: light green, white,
    red, green, tan
Glue
Nails
Hammer

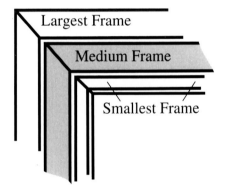

DIAGRAM

DIRECTIONS

1. Prepare the frames for painting.

2. Paint the largest frame light green; allow to dry.

3. Paint the medium frame white; allow to dry.

4. Paint the smallest frame red; allow to dry.

5. Measure and mark even intervals for placing the trees on the smallest frame.

6. Using tracing paper and a pencil, trace the tree pattern.

7. Refer to the photo and place the traced pattern on top of graphite paper on the smallest frame and retrace the design. (The graphite paper will transfer the design to the frame.)

8. Paint the trees green with tan stems; allow to dry.

9. Fit the frames inside one another. Use glue and/or nails to attach them.

HEART PATTERN

STAR PATTERN

TREE PATTERN

Pine Mirror

MATERIALS

One unfinished wood frame with
   2½"-wide flat-surfaced molding
½"-diameter wood punch
Hammer
Acrylic paint: rust
Walnut wood stain
Paintbrushes
Varnish
Tracing paper
Pencil
Tape
Newspaper
8" x 10" sheet of 18-gauge tooling
   copper
Tape
Ballpoint pen
Craft scissors
Epoxy glue
Soft cloth

DIRECTIONS

1. Hammer the wood punch into each corner of the frame in four places (Diagram 1).

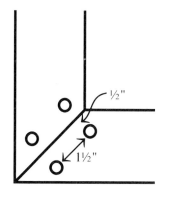

DIAGRAM 1

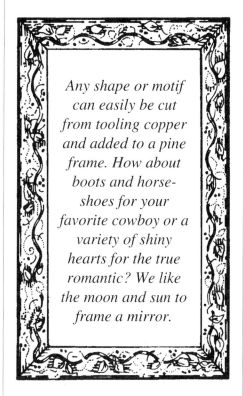

Any shape or motif can easily be cut from tooling copper and added to a pine frame. How about boots and horseshoes for your favorite cowboy or a variety of shiny hearts for the true romantic? We like the moon and sun to frame a mirror.

2. Prepare the frame for staining.

3. Dilute the rust paint with water and paint each punched round with the diluted paint.

4. Stain the frame with walnut wood stain, allowing the paint to bleed as desired. Allow to dry.

5. Apply two coats of varnish. Allow to dry.

6. Using tracing paper and a pencil, trace the patterns for the moon, sun, and star, including all details (page 118).

7. Place the tooling copper on several layers of newspaper.

8. Tape the sun, moon and star patterns to the copper. Using a ballpoint pen, retrace the designs with all the details to make one sun, one moon and seven stars. To complete the embossing, it may be necessary to trace the lines several times.

9. Cut out the designs, keeping the craft scissors deep in the cut and completing each cut before withdrawing them.

10. Glue the metal cutouts to the frame (see photo).

11. Wipe the metal with a soft cloth to remove pen or pencil marks.

Star

Sun

Moon

**PATTERNS FOR
PINE MIRROR**

118

Three Star Dolls

Three Star Dolls

MATERIALS
One frame with 7 ½" x 9 ½"
    window and flat surface
Three 4 ¼"-high doll-shaped wood
    cutouts
Tracing paper
Carbon paper
Pencil
Acrylic paints: light rust, dark rust,
    assorted other colors to decorate
    dolls
Paintbrushes
37 to 40 decorative upholstery tacks
Hammer
Spray gloss varnish
Glue

DIRECTIONS
Decorate the Dolls
1. Prepare the cutouts for painting.

2. Using tracing paper and a pencil, trace the patterns for the dolls' dresses (page 121).

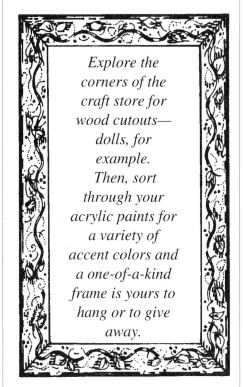

Explore the corners of the craft store for wood cutouts— dolls, for example. Then, sort through your acrylic paints for a variety of accent colors and a one-of-a-kind frame is yours to hang or to give away.

3. Place the carbon paper on top of the cutouts and then place the patterns on top of the carbon paper and retrace the patterns. (The carbon paper will transfer the designs to the cutouts.)

4. Paint the dolls' dresses any colors you like. Allow to dry.

Paint the Frame
1. Prepare the frame for painting.

2. Paint the frame in rust shades, blending from light on the top to dark on the bottom, mixing the two colors as desired; allow to dry.

3. Spray with two to three coats of varnish; allow to dry.

Complete the Finishing Touches
1. Hammer the upholstery tacks into the frame (see photo).

2. Position and glue the doll cutouts to the bottom edge of the frame, allowing ½" of the cutouts to extend below the bottom edge of the frame.

**THREE STAR DOLLS
PATTERNS**

Authorized by heirs of Pablo Picasso
Reinhold Enterprises LTD. N.Y. New York 1983

Picasso

Lilac Mood

MATERIALS

One wood frame with 16½" x 16½"
    window and 1½"-wide molding
13 yards of ½"-wide variegated
    lilac ribbon
Staple gun

DIRECTIONS

1. Staple one end of the ribbon to
the back of the frame.

2. Working with the whole length
of ribbon in your hand, wrap the
ribbon in a spiral pattern around the
entire frame, overlapping the edges
slightly (Diagram 1). Be sure to
keep the tension even and the
ribbon loose enough so that when
the mat board, art, and glass are
inserted, the ribbon is pressed into
the rabbet. Cut the ribbon and staple
the end to the back.

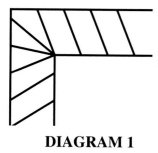

DIAGRAM 1

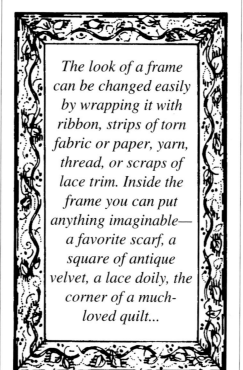

*The look of a frame
can be changed easily
by wrapping it with
ribbon, strips of torn
fabric or paper, yarn,
thread, or scraps of
lace trim. Inside the
frame you can put
anything imaginable—
a favorite scarf, a
square of antique
velvet, a lace doily, the
corner of a much-
loved quilt...*

3. Staple the end of the ribbon to the
back of the frame so that the ribbon
can be wrapped around the frame in
the opposite direction. Wrap in a
spiral pattern with 1" between
wraps (Diagram 2). The ribbon
should wrap easily around the
corners of the frame. Cover the
entire frame and staple the end to
the back.

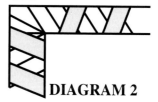

DIAGRAM 2

Sunflower Decoupage

MATERIALS
One unfinished frame
Paintbrush
Acrylic paint: peach
Wrapping paper or greeting cards
Scissors
Decoupage medium

DIRECTIONS
1. Prepare the frame for painting.

2. Paint the frame peach, allowing the wood grain to show through.

3. Cut out designs from wrapping paper or greeting cards.

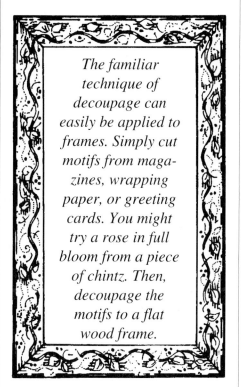

The familiar technique of decoupage can easily be applied to frames. Simply cut motifs from magazines, wrapping paper, or greeting cards. You might try a rose in full bloom from a piece of chintz. Then, decoupage the motifs to a flat wood frame.

4. Apply decoupage medium to the back of the designs and place them on the frame, wrapping the designs around the edges; trim excess.

5. Apply two coats of decoupage medium to the entire surface of the frame, following the manufacturer's directions.

Stamp by Numbers

MATERIALS

One 13½" x 15½" (outside dimensions) wood frame with 2½" wide flat surface (Diagram 1)

Long metal ruler

Medium weight watercolor paper

Tracing paper

Pencil

Graphite paper

Scissors

Two large artgum erasers

Craft knife

Paintbrushes: one flat, one fine tip

Acrylic paints: hot pink, red, purple gray, turquoise, green, peach, royal blue, medium blue, mint green, lavender

Scrap paper

Spray adhesive

Spray varnish

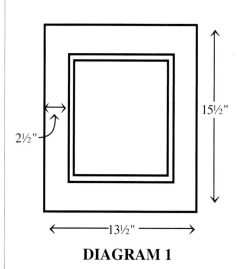

DIAGRAM 1

(Dimensions: 13½", 15½", 2½")

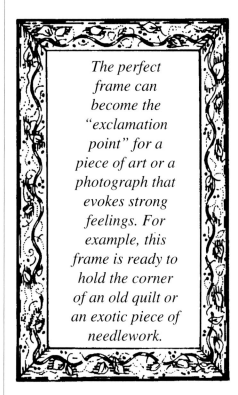

The perfect frame can become the "exclamation point" for a piece of art or a photograph that evokes strong feelings. For example, this frame is ready to hold the corner of an old quilt or an exotic piece of needlework.

DIRECTIONS

Prepare the Frame

1. Prepare the frame for painting.

2. Paint the frame hot pink.

Trace and Paint the Designs

1. Using ruler and a pencil, draw four strips of boxes on watercolor paper, as shown in Diagram 2.

2. Paint background colors in each box (Diagram 2); allow to dry.

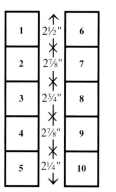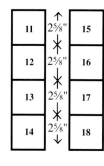

1	2½"	6		11	2⅝"	15
2	2⅞"	7		12	2⅝"	16
3	2¾"	8		13	2⅝"	17
4	2⅞"	9		14	2⅝"	18
5	2¼"	10				

1. Hot Pink   6. Peach   11. Lavender   15. Peach
2. Turquoise   7. Hot Pink   12. Mint Green   16. Turquoise
3. Lavender   8. Royal Blue   13. Royal Blue   17. Medium Blue
4. Royal Blue   9. Hot Pink   14. Red   18. Royal Blue
5. Red   10. Lavender

DIAGRAM 2

3. Using tracing paper and a pencil, trace Patterns 2 and 3 on page 129 and cut them out.

4. Place these patterns onto the artgum erasers and, using a craft knife, cut away edges around the patterns in the surface of the eraser to make raised pattern stamps.

5. Place a small amount of paint on the design stamps and stamp the two designs onto the A squares in Diagram 3. Pattern 2 is repeated four times in each block in which it is used. Pattern 3 is used once in one block and twice in another.

6. Using the end of an eraser dipped in paint, paint the B block (Diagram 3).

7. Using tracing paper and a pencil, trace the remaining patterns.

8. Place the traced patterns on graphite paper on top of the strips of boxes and retrace the correct design, as shown in Diagram 3, for all of the boxes not marked A, B, or C. (The graphite paper will transfer the designs to the boxes on the water-color paper.)

9. Using a fine-tipped paintbrush, paint the designs as necessary, filling in details to the stamped and traced patterns as desired.

10. Place paper over the designs in the boxes to mask off the two C squares and, using the technique shown in Diagram 4, splatter paint the C squares.

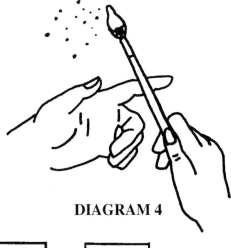

DIAGRAM 4

Complete the Finishing Touches

1. Dilute the peach paint to the consistency of ink.

2. Paint over the entire design surface. Allow to dry.

3. Trim the strips of boxes on the outside pencil lines, using a craft knife and metal ruler.

4. Use spray adhesive to attach the strips to the frame surface.

5. Spray the frame with one coat of varnish.

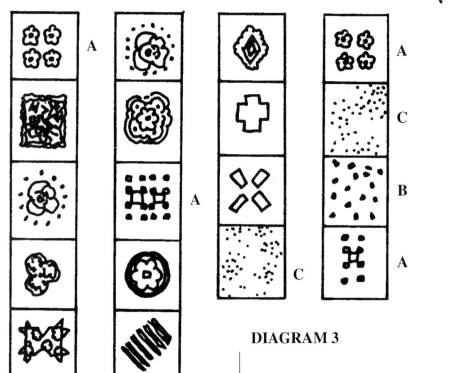

DIAGRAM 3

Stencilled Ivy

MATERIALS

One unfinished wood frame with
    8½" x 11½" window and a
    2⅜"-wide flat surface
One purchased stencil with 2"-wide
    pattern
Acrylic paint: cream
Tracing paper
Paintbrush
Masking tape
Scrap paper
Acrylic spray paint: yellow,
    medium green, dark green
Acrylic matte spray finish

DIRECTIONS

1. Prepare the frame for painting.

2. Paint the frame cream, using two coats, if needed. Allow to dry.

3. Tape the stencil to the frame.

4. Cover the remainder of the frame with paper.

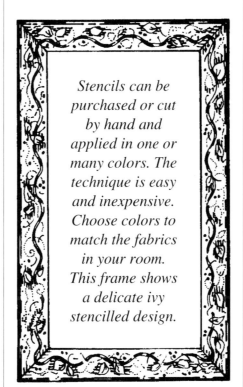

Stencils can be purchased or cut by hand and applied in one or many colors. The technique is easy and inexpensive. Choose colors to match the fabrics in your room. This frame shows a delicate ivy stencilled design.

5. Spray paint lightly over the design, using yellow first, then medium green, and finally, a light coat of dark green. Allow paint to dry before removing the stencil.

6. Place the stencil on another part of the frame and repeat Steps 4 and 5 until you have completed decorating the frame. Adjust the stencil as needed so that it works well in the corners. Use masking tape to delete sections of the stencil where desired.

7. After the stencilled design is completed and dried, spray entire frame with two coats of acrylic finish. Allow to dry.

Contemporary Butler

MATERIALS

One frame with 19½" x 13½" window
Wrapping paper or wallpaper
One 20" x 14" piece of glass
One 20" x 14" piece of ⅛" Masonite
Acrylic paints: purple, orange, blue
Four 1¾"-wide wooden balls
Four 1½"-wide wooden balls
Two 8" pieces of ⅞" wide dowel
Twelve ½"-long pieces of ¼"-wide dowel
Wood glue
Drill and ¼" bit
Spray semi-gloss varnish
Small nails
Spray adhesive
One 20" x 14" piece of foam board

DIRECTIONS

1. Prepare frame for painting. Paint with two coats of purple. Allow to dry.

Moldings and finials come in so many shapes and finishes that the possibilities for trays and handles are endless. Explore marbleizing and sponge painting, gold leafing or splatter painting for the finish on yours.

2. Drill ¼" deep holes as follows: one in top and bottom of each 1¾" wooden ball; one in each 1½" wooden ball; one in each end of 8" dowels. Also drill pairs of ¼" deep holes centered and 5½" apart on one side of the 8" dowels and the short ends of the frame.

3. Prepare dowels and balls for painting. Paint dowels with two coats of blue; paint balls with two coats of orange. Allow to dry.

4. To assemble handles, place a drop of glue in each hole and insert small dowel pegs (Diagram 1).

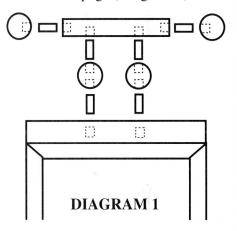

DIAGRAM 1

5. Spray all surfaces of frame with two or three coats of varnish.

6. With frame face down, insert glass. Trim paper to 20" x 14", placing pattern as desired. Using spray adhesive, attach paper to foam board. Insert in frame with design facing glass. Insert Masonite. Secure with nails.

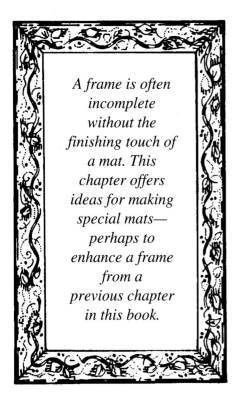

A frame is often incomplete without the finishing touch of a mat. This chapter offers ideas for making special mats— perhaps to enhance a frame from a previous chapter in this book.

Chapter Three

Baseball Collage Mat

MATERIALS

Mat board with multiple oval
   windows
Baseball photos cut from magazines
   and newspapers (or other items)
Craft knife
Glue

DIRECTIONS

1. Trim photos (or other items) and
arrange them over the entire surface
of the mat board, obscuring the
windows. The composition will
vary depending on the shape and
size of the items.

*Collage mats can be
made to match the
photo being framed.
We've used baseball
cards and photos for
this mat, making it
perfect for a special
fan. But, you can
make a collage with
almost anything. Use
magazines, old greet-
ing cards, photos,
pieces of fabric or
lace—anything
that's flat.*

2. Glue the items in place. Allow to
dry.

3. Turn the mat face down on a
protected surface.

4. Trim the collage to open the oval
windows.

Doily Mats

Rectangular Mat
MATERIALS

One 8½" x 5½" white paper doily
    with oval patterned center
One 9" x 6" cream mat board
Pencil
Craft knife
Spray adhesive

DIRECTIONS

1. Carefully cut oval center from the doily following embossed design.

2. Center the doily on the mat board and trace the oval opening onto the mat board.

3. Cut the oval window in the mat board.

4. Spray the back side of the doily with adhesive and place the doily over the mat board, matching windows.

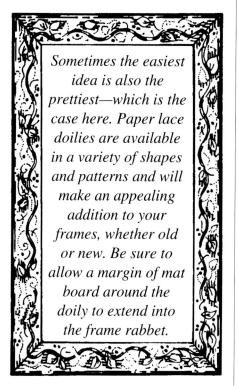

Sometimes the easiest idea is also the prettiest—which is the case here. Paper lace doilies are available in a variety of shapes and patterns and will make an appealing addition to your frames, whether old or new. Be sure to allow a margin of mat board around the doily to extend into the frame rabbet.

Diamond Mat
MATERIALS

One 12" x 12" white paper doily
One 12½" x 12½" light blue mat
    board
Pencil
Craft knife
Spray adhesive

DIRECTIONS

1. Position the doily to form a diamond and carefully cut a square in the center, leaving at least 1" between the corners of the square and the edge of the doily.

2. Place the doily on the mat board and trace the square opening onto the mat board.

3. Cut the square window in the mat board.

4. Spray the back side of the doily with adhesive and place the doily over the mat board, matching windows.

Cross-Stitch Garland Mat

MATERIALS

One 8" x 10" purchased mat with
4½" x 6½" window
Completed cross-stitch design (see
pattern and instructions)
One 8" x 10" piece of fleece
Spray adhesive
Dressmaker's pen

DIRECTIONS

1. Complete the cross-stitch design
on amaretto Murano 30.

2. Spray adhesive on the mat.

3. Place the fleece over the mat and
trim the fleece from the window and
edges, as needed.

4. Center the mat on the wrong side
of the cross-stitch fabric and, using
dressmaker's pen, trace the outline
of the mat onto the fabric.

*Add a soft texture
to your mat with
the floss and
fabric of a
cross-stitch
design.
Your handwork
will underscore
your message
of love
and caring.*

5. Cut a window 1½" inside the
traced line. Clip the corners nearly
to the mat. Wrap the fabric around
the window to the back and glue.
Wrap the fabric on the outside
edges to the back and glue, trimming any excess from the corners as
needed.

To Complete Cross-Stitch Design

Cross-stitch on amaretto Murano 30
over two threads. The finished
design is 7¼" x 9⅜". Cut the fabric
14" x 16".

Anchor		DMC (used for sample)	
		Step 1: Cross-stitch (2 strands)	
891	ı	676	Old Gold-lt.
307	∴	783	Christmas Gold
50	□	3716	Wild Rose-lt.
75	■	3733	Dusty Rose-lt.
108	○	211	Lavender-lt.
117	·	341	Blue Violet-lt.
158	●	828	Blue-ultra vy. lt.
214	△	368	Pistachio Green-lt.
212	✕	561	Jade-vy. dk.
393	▲	3790	Beige Gray-ultra vy. dk.
		Step 2: Backstitch (1 strand)	
212		561	Jade-vy. dk.

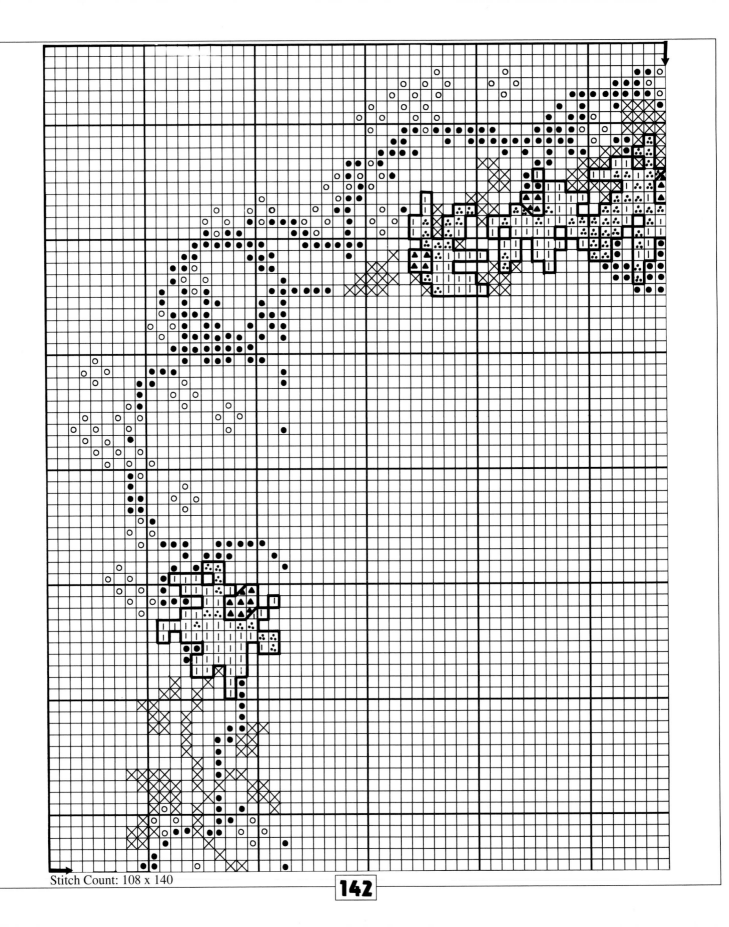

Stitch Count: 108 x 140

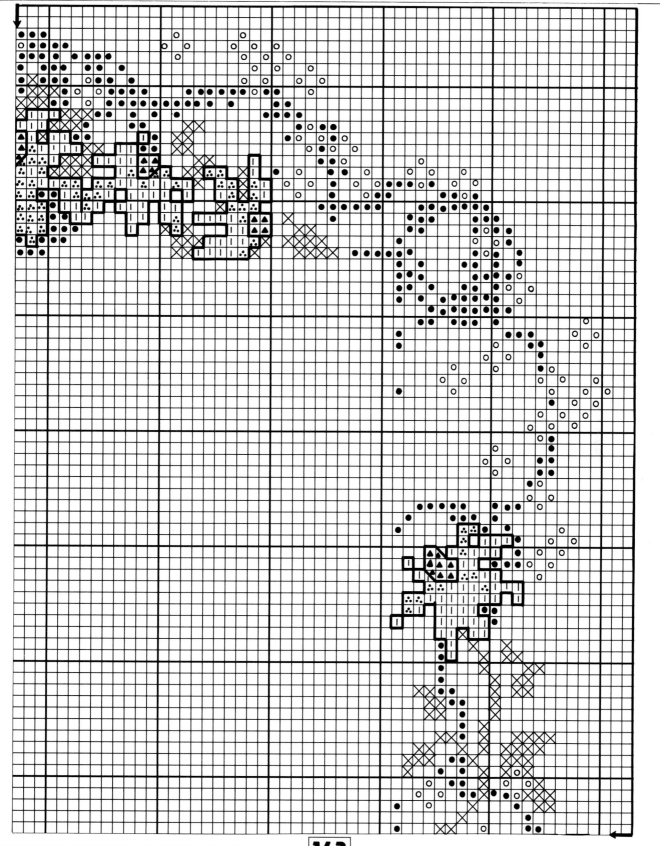

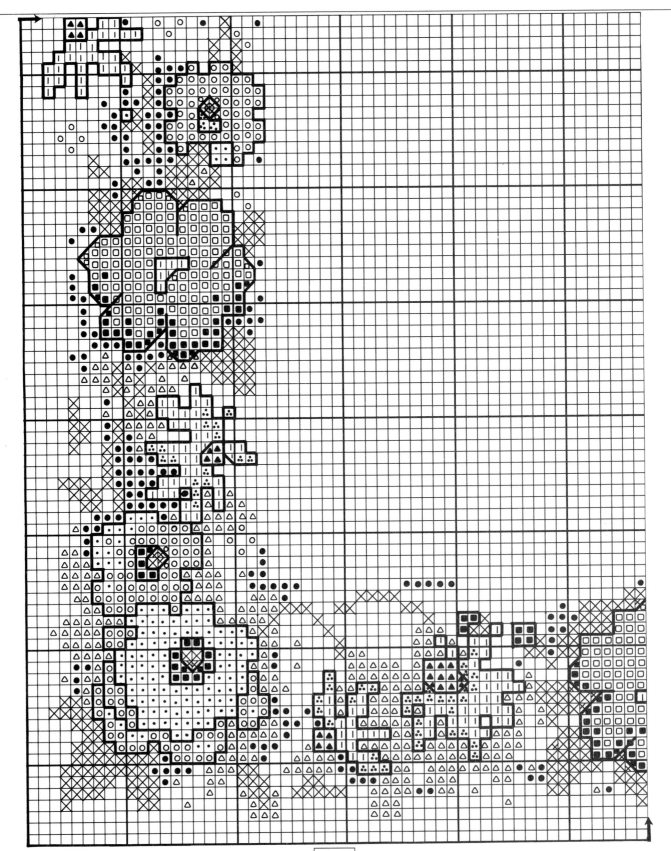

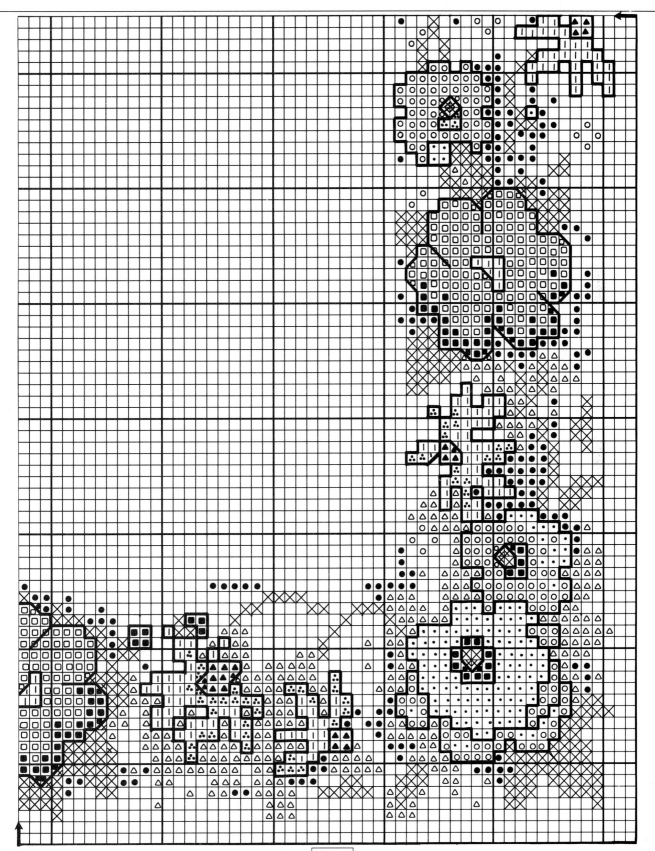

A Small Delight

MATERIALS

Fabric with decorative weave: one
    10" x 12" piece and one
    3¼" x 3¼" piece
Fabric stiffener
Acrylic paint: white
Paintbrush
Waxed paper
Twigs: two 2" long and four 3" long
¾"-wide craft bird nest with eggs
Small craft bird
Seven cream satin roses
⅝ yard of ⅛"-wide ivory satin ribbon
Fine gold wire
Scissors
Glue
8" x 8" mat board

DIRECTIONS

1. Round the corners of the 3¼" x 3¼" piece of fabric. (You may use a small round plate as a guide when trimming the fabric corners.)

2. Dip the fabric in stiffener. Shape it according to Diagram 1. Allow it to dry on waxed paper.

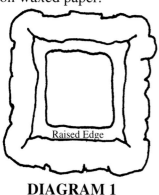

Raised Edge

DIAGRAM 1

The tiny piece of fabric shown here surrounded by twigs and other natural finds could also be shaped into a heart and embellished with lace or jewelry or ornaments. A mat with a dimensional element like this works best in a shadowbox frame.

3. Paint the twigs with several coats of white; allow to dry.

4. Glue the twigs together (Diagram 2).

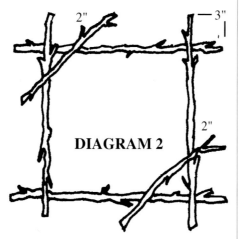

2"

3"

2"

DIAGRAM 2

5. Glue the satin roses, the bird, and the nest to the twigs (Diagram 3).

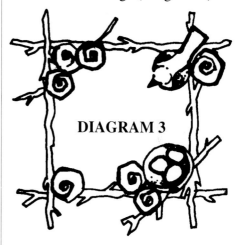

DIAGRAM 3

6. Wind the length of gold wire around the ivory satin ribbon. Using glue, secure one end of the ribbon in the top left corner of the twig square.

7. Loosely wind the wire/ribbon around the twigs and then secure the other end of the ribbon in the opposite corner.

8. Glue twig frame onto the shaped fabric. Center and trim art to fit inside twig frame window. Glue.

9. Center the mat board over the wrong side of the large piece of woven fabric, wrap the fabric to the back of the mat, and glue the edges.

10. Center and glue the shaped fabric square with the twigs onto the covered mat.

Appliquéd Bear & Friends

MATERIALS

One pre-cut purchased 8" x 10" mat
    with 4½" x 6½" oval window
14" x 16" green fabric for
    background
Tracing paper
Pencil
Scissors
Compass
Dressmaker's pen
Assorted scraps of fabric in
    different colors: pink, lavender,
    coordinating small prints
Threads to match
Embroidery floss: pink, lavender,
    yellow
8" x 10" piece of fleece
Spray adhesive

DIRECTIONS

Make and Appliqué the Designs

1. Using tracing paper and a pencil, trace the patterns for the sun, basket, basket goodies, kite, kite tail, heart, sock, scalloped flower, flower center, house, roof, ice cream cone, ice cream scoop, car, car window, car wheels, butterfly wings, and butterfly body, as well as bear's head, arms, hand, dress, legs, and basket on pages 150 and 151. Cut the patterns out.

2. Place the patterns on right side of scrap fabric and, adding ⅛" seam allowance to all edges of all pieces,

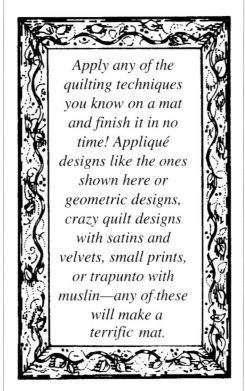

Apply any of the quilting techniques you know on a mat and finish it in no time! Appliqué designs like the ones shown here or geometric designs, crazy quilt designs with satins and velvets, small prints, or trapunto with muslin—any of these will make a terrific mat.

mark three kite tails, two scalloped flowers, two flower centers, two socks, and one of each other pattern. Cut out.

3. Center and, using dressmaker's pen, trace the mat outer edges and window edges onto the right side of the green background fabric.

4. Place the appliqué pieces on the fabric, layering as needed (see photo and Steps 6, 7, and 8).

5. To appliqué, turn under the seam allowance as you go, slipstitching the folded edge to the backing with

matching thread. On inside curves, clip the seam allowance almost to the folded edge as needed. Trim excess fabric from tips and corners to eliminate bulk. Use tiny, even stitches, about ⅛" apart, using smaller stitches as needed on inside curves and sharp points.

6. Working clockwise from the top, appliqué the sun, basket, and three round flowers. Then, appliqué the kite and heart.

7. Trace the outline for the bear's dress onto the backing and set dress aside. Note that the broken lines of the dress indicate where it overlaps other pieces. Position the arms and the legs and appliqué. Appliqué the dress, then the head, hand, and basket.

8. Appliqué the socks and one scalloped flower; add a round flower for the center.

9. Appliqué the house, then the roof; ice cream, then cone; scalloped flower and center; car, then window and wheels; butterfly wings, then body.

10. Embellish with embroidery, using two strands of floss. With pink floss, sew a running stitch ⅛" outside the scalloped flowers and satin stitch the door of the house and the bear nose. Also with pink floss, make two French knots for the bear's eyes, using two strands and one wrap.

11. With lavender floss, backstitch the butterfly antennae and the heels and the toes of the socks. Also, with lavender floss, satin stitch the windows of the house and sew a running stitch for the kite tail, securing three tail pieces in stitches with a small tuck.

12. With yellow floss, outline stitch the sun's rays.

Make the Mat

1. Trim the fleece ¼" smaller than the mat on the outside edges and extending ¼" inside the window.

2. With spray adhesive, attach the fleece to the mat.

3. Center the green background fabric with the appliqué designs over the fleece side of the mat.

4. Trim the background fabric to 1" larger than the mat on all outside edges and the window. Clip the inside edges at ½" intervals. Wrap them to the back of the mat and glue, trimming any excess from the corners. Wrap the outside edges of the fabric to the back side of the mat and glue.

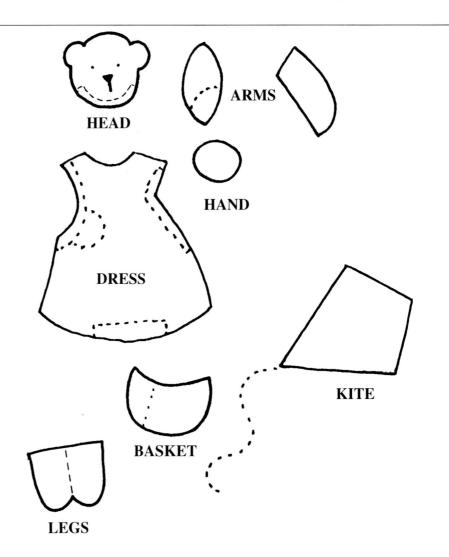

HEAD

ARMS

HAND

DRESS

KITE

BASKET

LEGS

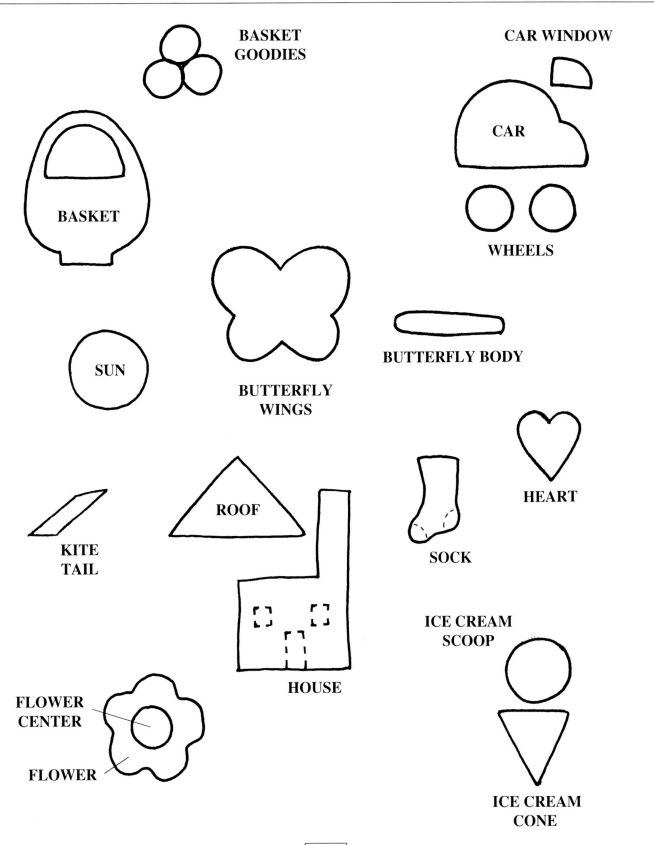

BASKET
GOODIES

CAR WINDOW

BASKET

CAR

WHEELS

SUN

BUTTERFLY
WINGS

BUTTERFLY BODY

HEART

KITE
TAIL

ROOF

SOCK

HOUSE

ICE CREAM
SCOOP

FLOWER
CENTER

FLOWER

ICE CREAM
CONE

Woven Paper Mat

MATERIALS
11" x 14" mat board with window
Decorative papers: natural, green, lavender
Craft knife and metal ruler
15" x 18" or larger corrugated cardboard or foam board for work surface
Scissors
Straight pins
Spray adhesive
Tracing paper
Pencil
Tape
Glue

DIRECTIONS
1. Cut a 5" x 8" window in the mat board (Diagram 1).

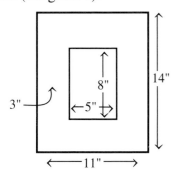

DIAGRAM 1

2. With a craft knife and metal ruler, cut twenty-five 13" x ½" strips of green paper and three 13" x ½" strips of natural paper.

3. Arrange the strips of paper side by side horizontally on the

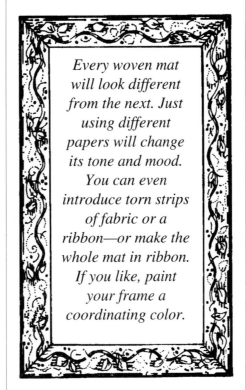

Every woven mat will look different from the next. Just using different papers will change its tone and mood. You can even introduce torn strips of fabric or a ribbon—or make the whole mat in ribbon. If you like, paint your frame a coordinating color.

cardboard, pinning the left end of each strip.

4. Cut nineteen 16" x ½" strips of lavender paper and three 16" x ½" strips of natural paper.

5. Arrange these strips vertically over the first layer on the cardboard (Diagram 2), pinning the top end of each strip.

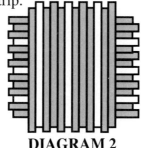

DIAGRAM 2

6. Weave the strips together, being careful not to tear the paper. Additional pins may be needed to secure pieces while weaving. After weaving is complete, remove the pins.

7. Spray mat board with adhesive. Keeping the strips at right angles, place the woven piece on the mat. Wrap the woven edges to the back of the mat and secure with tape.

8. Turn the mat board over and cut 1" inside the window, all the way around. Wrap the woven edges to the wrong side and secure with tape.

9. Using tracing paper and a pencil, trace heart patterns and cut out.

10. Place the heart patterns on natural paper; trace and cut out one large and three small hearts.

11. Glue the hearts onto the woven mat (see photo).

LARGE HEART

SMALL HEART

Metal Mats

Gracefully Aged Copper
MATERIALS (three-window mat)

One 3" x 36" piece of $^1/32$" balsa wood
One 13" x 6½" piece of mat board
Three 4" x 6" pieces of 18 gauge tooling copper
Rotary cutter, mat, and straight edge
Scissors for cutting metal
Acrylic paint: brown
Paintbrush
Wood glue
Newspapers
Ballpoint pen
Copper patina
Strapping tape
Double-sided tape

DIRECTIONS

1. Using rotary cutter, cut two ½" x 6½" strips, two ¾" x 6½" strips, and two ¾" x 13" strips from balsa wood.

2. Paint the strips brown; allow to dry.

3. Using wood glue, glue the strips as shown in Diagram 1.

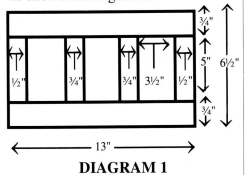

DIAGRAM 1

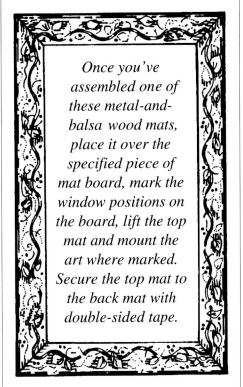

Once you've assembled one of these metal-and-balsa wood mats, place it over the specified piece of mat board, mark the window positions on the board, lift the top mat and mount the art where marked. Secure the top mat to the back mat with double-sided tape.

4. Make three copies of the mat pattern on page 159 on a photocopy machine. Center and tape the pattern to each copper piece.

5. Stack newspaper to provide a padded work surface and place the copper pieces with the patterns on them on this work surface.

6. Using a ballpoint pen, retrace the pattern lines, pressing firmly. Also mark the window. You may need to repeat the lines to make the impressions deep enough. (The embossed pattern will be reversed on the copper.)

7. Following the lines, cut a window in each of the three pieces of copper.

8. Apply copper patina, following manufacturer's instructions. Allow to dry.

9. Center the copper mats behind the balsa wood grid. Secure with strapping tape.

Victorian Parlor
MATERIALS (four-window mat)

One 3" x 36" piece of $^1/32$" balsa wood
One 9" x 10" piece of mat board
Four 4½" x 5" pieces of 36 gauge tooling aluminum
Rotary cutter, mat, and straight edge
Scissors for cutting metal
Acrylic paint: brown
Paintbrush
Wood glue
Ballpoint pen
Newspapers
Strapping tape

DIRECTIONS

1. Using the rotary cutter, cut one ½" x 9" strip and one ½" x 10" strip from the balsa wood.

2. Paint the strips brown; allow to dry.

3. With wood glue, glue the strips together (Diagram 1).

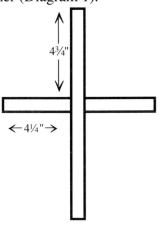

4¾"

←—4¼"—→

DIAGRAM 1

4. Make four copies of mat pattern on page 159 on a photocopy machine.

5. Center and tape the pattern to each aluminum piece.

6. Stack newspaper to provide a padded work surface and place the aluminum pieces with the patterns on them on this work surface.

7. Using a ballpoint pen, retrace the pattern lines, pressing firmly. Also mark the window. You may need to repeat the lines to make the impressions deep enough. (The embossed pattern will be reversed on the aluminum.)

8. Following the lines, cut a window in each of the four pieces of aluminum.

9. Center the aluminum mats behind the balsa wood grid and secure with strapping tape.

Embellished Copper
MATERIALS (for nine-window mat, page 158)
One 3" x 36" piece of ¹/₃₂" balsa wood
One 10½" x 14⅝" piece of mat board
Nine 3½" x 4⅞" pieces of 36 gauge tooling copper
Rotary cutter, mat, and straight edge
Scissors for cutting metal
Acrylic paint: brown
Paintbrush
Wood glue
Ballpoint pen
Newspapers
Strapping tape

DIRECTIONS
1. Using the rotary cutter, cut two ½" x 14⅝" strips and two ½" x 10½" strips from the balsa wood.

2. Paint the strips brown; allow to dry.

3. With wood glue, glue the strips together (Diagram 1).

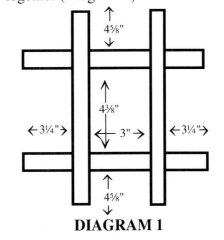

4⅝"

4⅜"

←—3¼"—→   ←—3"—→   ←—3¼"—→

4⅝"

DIAGRAM 1

4. Make four copies of one mat pattern and five copies of the other mat pattern on page 159 on a photocopy machine.

5. Center and tape the patterns to each copper piece.

6. Stack newspapers to provide a padded work surface and place the copper pieces with the patterns on them on this work surface.

7. Using a ballpoint pen, retrace the pattern lines, pressing firmly. Also mark the window. You may need to repeat the lines to make the impressions deep enough. (The embossed pattern will be reversed on the copper.)

8. Following the lines, cut a window in each of the nine pieces of copper.

9. Center the copper mats behind the balsa wood grid. Secure with strapping tape.

METAL MAT
PATTERNS

Nine Window

Four Window

Three Window

Nine Window

159

Naturally Nice Mat

MATERIALS

One white 13" x 15½" mat board
Craft knife
Acrylic paint: brown
Wide-toothed comb
Glue
Collage materials: small pieces of
    torn cream rice paper, small
    pieces of torn white rice paper,
    ⅛"-wide paper strips, string, 1"
    to 2" strips of bark, 1 small
    pressed maple leaf, white
    pressed flowers, white straw
    flowers, seven ⅜"-wide shells,
    dark brown beads, 7" piece of
    natural spun wool

DIRECTIONS

1. Cut a 3½" x 6" window in the
mat board (Diagram 1).

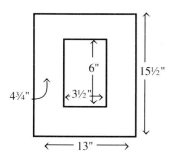

DIAGRAM 1

*If you are a
lover of dried
flowers and
handmade
paper, this
display of
summer's
treasures will
find a perfect
place in your
home and
heart.*

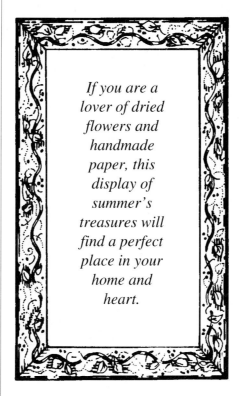

2. Dip the comb in the brown paint
and make a pattern on the mat
board (Diagram 2); allow to dry.

DIAGRAM 2

3. Arrange and glue the collage
materials to the mat board in the
sequence given in the Materials list
(see photo).

Yo-Yo Mat

MATERIALS

One 12½" x 12½" piece of mat
    board
Paper
Compass
Pencil
Scissors
½ yard of raspberry fabric
Scraps of 15 different fabrics:
    melon, matte lavender, shiny
    lavender, pink, antique mauve,
    rose, dusty rose, raspberry, dark
    brown, pale rose, light brown,
    chocolate milk, taupe, cream,
    champagne
Needle and mauve thread
12½" x 12½" piece of cardboard for
    backing
Dressmaker's pen
Fabric glue

DIRECTIONS
Make the Yo-Yos

1. Using a compass and pencil,
draw a 2½"-diameter circle onto
paper for a yo-yo pattern. Cut the
pattern out.

2. Place the pattern on a fabric
scrap and cut out a round piece of
fabric.

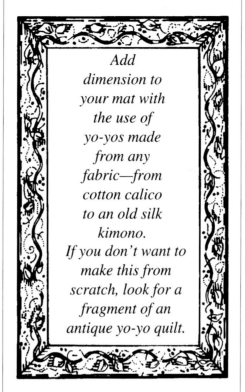

Add dimension to your mat with the use of yo-yos made from any fabric—from cotton calico to an old silk kimono. If you don't want to make this from scratch, look for a fragment of an antique yo-yo quilt.

3. Fold in the edge of the fabric
circle ¼" and finger press (Diagram
1). With a needle and one strand of
thread, sew a running stitch near the
folded edge (Diagram 2).

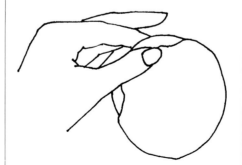

DIAGRAM 1

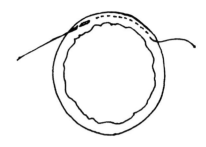

DIAGRAM 2

4. Gather the edge and press flat
with gathered edges centered
(Diagram 3). Secure the ends of the
gathering threads and tuck inside
yo-yo.

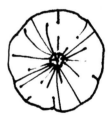

DIAGRAM 3

5. Repeat Steps 2, 3, and 4 to make
a total of 160 yo-yos, referring to
the following table for the number
of each color.

Index